UNDERCOVER AMISH

Ashley Emma

Like free eBooks?

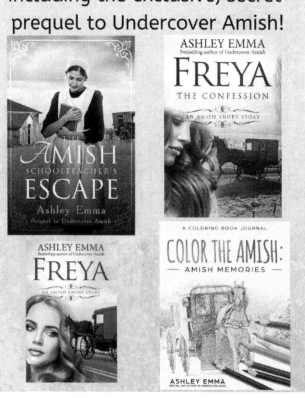

Free Short Story!

FREYA: AN AMISH SHORT STORY (Book 1 in the Freya Series)

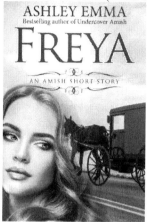

Get Freya here on Amazon for free or search Amazon for "Freya by Ashley Emma": https://www.amazon.com/Freya-Amish-Short-Ashley-Emma-ebook/dp/B01MSP03UX

Other books by Ashley Emma on Amazon

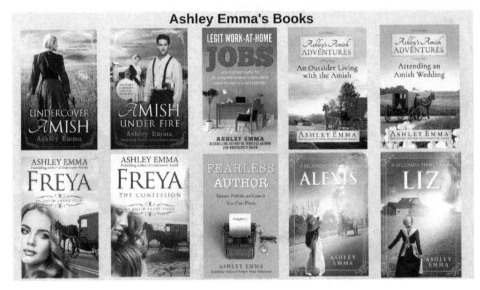

Coming 2019:

COMING AUTUMN 2018: AMISH AMNESIA

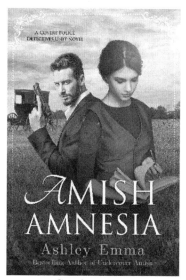

Coming soon:
Freya (Book 3)
Amish Twin Sisters
The Ring Thief

Check out my author Facebook page at
www.facebook.com/AshleyEmmaAuthor to see rare photos from
when I lived with the Amish in Unity, Maine

Table of Contents

Don't forget to download free Amish books at
http://www.ashleyemmaauthor.com!

Praise for *Undercover Amish*

"*Undercover Amish* is the first Amish novel I've read, and I have to say it was a fascinating and insightful look into a different culture. Ashley Emma clearly did extensive research on the subject and portrayed this group in a compassionate, thoughtful manner. Couple her careful handling of this society with her compelling characters and heart-racing plot, and you've got a real winner!"

-Staci Troilo, author of *Mind Control, Bleeding Heart* and many other titles

"What can I say, I LOVE mysteries! I love getting to know the characters, their motivations and then trying to figure out the outcomes. I am therefore delighted to have discovered *Undercover Amish*. Not only does the main character, Olivia, has a unique background of being Amish, but the trajectory of her life from that background to becoming a policewoman is fascinating and totally unexpected. Not only did I find myself engrossed in the unraveling of a crime, but also in the learning about a culture, within my own country, about which I was, admittedly, basically ignorant. Kudos to Ashley Emma for creating this wonderful series. I can't wait to read more of them!"

-Leslie K. Malin, LCSW, psychotherapist, iLife Transition Coach, and author of *Cracked Open: Reflections on the Transformative Power of Failure, Fear, & Doubt* website/blog: http://www.JustThinkn.com

"*Undercover Amish* is a suspenseful, realistic work of fiction. Ashley weaves two opposite worlds together in a fast-paced story following Detective Olivia Mast. Olivia's journey forces her to face issues of identity, rise up to work challenges, and eventually she finds love. It's an easy read that will keep you guessing until the end."
-J.P. Sterling, author of *Ruby in the Water*

"Buy this book! It's a five-star read in my opinion. Whether you have ever read Amish detective stories before or not, I know you'll like this one and be totally engaged from start to finish. The characters are well-developed, unique, quirky, and three-dimensional. I enjoyed the author giving her readers an inside view of the Amish community, especially during dangerous and unpredictable times. I eagerly await the sequel to this novel!"
-Wendy Pearson, moderator of *The Write Practice*

"I love a good mystery and this one has an interesting storyline. A relatively short read and kept me engaged and trying to guess the next twist. This is the kind of book I love to have when traveling or for an afternoon at the beach."
-C.L. Ferrari, bestselling author of *Enriching Your Retirement*

"Ashley Emma has crafted an intriguing crime mystery with a surprising twist. I didn't see that ending coming at all. And I'm a little jealous. Once I got into this book, I couldn't put it down."

2

-Michael Wilkinson, bestselling author of *A Father's Guide to Raising Daughters*

"I really enjoyed this book, right through the last page!! *Undercover Amish* is a compelling read that will keep you going until the very end! The only disappointing thing for me about *Undercover Amish* was when the story ended—I already miss the main characters!"
-Sue M Wilson, author of *Home Matters*
www.suemwilson.com

"This book will take no time at all to grab you and take you into a world most of us know nothing about. Because the author spent time with the Amish, Ashley Emma is able to present her story in a truthful manner. After you read this, you will feel as though you know enough to say you understand them. (You may even find yourself wanting to wear more solids.) But murder has crept into their safe haven. Olivia, the main character, who was once Amish comes back and investigates a string of crimes, all while being undercover. I highly recommend this book. Ashley keeps you on the edge of your horse and buggy seat while making you fall in love with her characters. You'll be sorry once it is over. Thankfully there are more of her books to read coming soon!"
-Emily L. Pittsford, author of *A Most Incredible Witness*

"Don't let the word "Amish" fool you, with more than one twist at the end, this book is very riveting. I didn't want to put it down. I've been looking for a new author to read for a while, so glad I found Ashley Emma. Can't wait for her next one."

-Karen Herzog, court transcript proofreader
http://www.ProofIsInTheReading.com

Praise for *Ashley's Amish Adventures*

"A refreshing glimpse inside Ashley Emma's writing process. Reading about her in-depth, genuine curiosity and appreciation for the people she met on her adventure into the Amish community felt like an intimate behind-the-scenes tour."

--Marie Schaeller, bestselling author of *Breaking the Chains of Silence*

http://www.Marieschaeller.com

"Emma Ashley is a brilliant author. I admire her work. I was wondering what it is like to be Amish and also what it is like to be inside an Amish community. Through her books, she leads the readers into an unknown environment. She does it in a way that does not make me feel lost or left all by myself. She holds the reader's hand all along through the story. Therefore, I recommend you to get a tour with Emma Ashley in her Amish world."

--Ndeye Labadens, multi-bestselling author of *African Memories: Travels into the Interior of Africa, Secrets Book Launch Journey to the Ultimate Success, Relocation without Dislocation: Make New Friends, Keep the Old, and Australian Memories: Discover the Aussie Land and the Mysterious Red Center*

"An intriguing and riveting read! This book gives readers a very rare peek into life in an Amish community. The author personally

immersed herself into the Amish life, in order to authentically portray their passion for contentment, simplicity, and faith as the setting for an adventure of a lifetime. While it is an easy read, it is very intriguing and riveting! The author has a way of drawing a reader into every scene and keeping the momentum going. The characters she introduces us to are so real and relatable, despite the fact that they live such distinct lives from what would be considered main stream modern America! In fact, there is a sense of envy that causes an inevitable reflection on what we consider to be necessary and essential in our daily lives. It was a refreshing read!"
--Tracy Lee, author and pastor

"I LOVE these Amish books by Ashley Emma. They not only grab your interest and keep you reading, they give you a feel like you know a few Amish people and care about them. This is the most powerful step to understanding a culture different from your own. Thanks, Ashley, you have broadened my horizons and you made it fun on the way! There is also a homespun gentleness and honesty about the spiritual side of these differences. If everyone acted like this, Christianity would have a better world view and there would be less hatred in the world. There is nothing more we could ask for from a few books!"

--Chris McKay Pierce, author of *Customer Service can be Murder*

Acknowledgements for Undercover Amish

I first of all want to thank God for giving me a love of writing, which began when I was a child. He has set me on this journey full of ups and downs, including eleven years of writing books and making writing mistakes that have gotten me where I am now. It has been a long road, but finally, the first of several of my books has been published and my dreams have come true!

I also want to thank my husband David who has cheered me up when things got difficult and encouraged me when I thought my books would be a failure. He has been on board with me from the beginning and is always by my side!

Thank you to my parents, the most generous people I know! Thank you to my dad for building our house and to my mom for being a saintly mother to all six of us kids. She home schooled us and brought me to dance practices and encouraged all of us to follow our dreams. She was the one who first got me interested in the Amish when she let me borrow some of her Amish romance novels. My mom was also the one who came with me when I went to live with the Amish for the first time. She is the kind of person who will drop everything to help someone when they call, and I hope I can be as generous as my parents one day.

Thank you to Scott Evans, my brother-in-law, who is a police officer, for answering all my questions about police procedures and crime scene investigations.

Thank you to these particular beta readers who gave me valuable feedback that greatly improved this manuscript: Ethan Musser, Wendy Pearson, Peggy Lowell, C.L. Ferarri, Eve Foreman, Sue Wilson, Brittany Nidds, and Jen Mikesell. Thank you so much for your suggestions!

And thank you to these awesome proofreaders in my Facebook circle of proofreaders who found all those sneaky typos: Sharon Ferrell, Staci Troilo, Rachel Boice, Lisa Incarnato, Kelly Polvi, Suzette May, Diana Smith Busby, and Megan Romania.

A BIG thank you to Stacy Claflin, Kathy Ide and Carol J. Post, three amazing authors who answered so many of my questions over email. I hope that one day I will be half the writers you are and that I can pass down what I have learned to someone who will appreciate it like you did for me. I've never met any of you in person but I am so grateful to you for teaching me so much! Thank you, Carol, for reading and critiquing the book! You'll never know how much I appreciate it.

Thank you to Stephanie Blore and Marilize Roos for reading this book, helping me tweak certain parts and making it is so much better! I appreciate your help and feedback so much.

Also a big thank you to my Amish friends in Unity, Maine, who let me stay with them and befriend them as I did research for this novel. They are some of the kindest people I've ever met and I truly do admire them.

Author's Note and Some Information about the Amish

Thank you for reading *Undercover Amish: A Covert Police Detectives Novel*. I had a lot of fun spending time with the Amish of Unity, Maine, for this series when I was twenty years old. I wrote this book (and a few other Amish novels coming soon) shortly after.

I wrote two books that describe when I lived with their community for several days in my series *Ashley's Amish Adventures*. If you are curious about what it would be like to live with the Amish, I bet you would like these books!

Many people have preconceived notions about the Amish that are just not true, thanks to unrealistic novels and TV shows. There are numerous communities scattered across the USA, and there are also some in Canada. Each of them are unique and have different rules.

For example, many people might think that the Amish speak very formally, but in Maine they talk just like you and me when they are speaking English. Some of the houses do have an outlet for charging battery-operated devices. Also, they eat food that one would not think is Amish, like taco casseroles. They ride bikes, but they don't play instruments. They shop in stores to buy things like toothpaste, perfume, hair elastics, crackers, and cereal.

They have first names that don't always sound very Amish, and "dating" and "courting" mean the same thing to them. They do not use electricity, but they do have indoor toilets. The Amish are known for being pacifists, and they do not report crimes within their community. They are against answering questions from the police about those crimes. They believe that they should forgive and move on, and they believe that vengeance is the Lord's, no matter what.

A few of these things might differ for other Amish communities, such as the Amish of Lancaster County, because I based this novel on the Amish of Maine. They are a really awesome group of people! They are very friendly, outgoing, and approachable. They welcomed me, a total stranger, into their homes and befriended me. They were also happy that I was doing my research before writing this book.

Covert Police Detectives Unit is a fictional branch in Maine made of police officers, detectives, special agents and bodyguards who all work together. In the upcoming books in this series, you will meet characters who work in the different departments of CPDU.

I do hope you enjoy this story! If you enjoyed it, I would appreciate an honest review on Amazon so other readers can see what you thought of the book. Here is the link.

Please visit http://ashleyemmaauthor.com to download some of my books for free and join my email list so you can be the first to know about new book releases. You can also become a beta reader—one of the first people to read my new books—and get them all for free!

If you want to see photos from my Amish adventure, check out my author Facebook page. Also, I love to hear from my readers. Please feel free to email me at amishbookwriter@gmail.com or ashley@ashleyemmaauthor.com and we can chat!

Happy reading!

Ashley Emma

Chapter One

"Did you find everything you were looking for?" Jake asked.

Olivia Sullivan looked up to see her husband staring at her with furrowed brows and narrowed eyes. The anger flickering in them would soon grow into a hungry flame. He wouldn't yell at her here in the grocery store, but she should hurry to avoid a lecture later at home.

For a moment, she pondered his question. Had she found everything she was looking for?

No.

This was not the life she had signed up for when she had made her vows to Jake Sullivan.

"Olivia? Did you hear me?" His voice, low and menacing, came through clenched teeth.

"Sorry. I just need to find some toothpaste. I'll be right back."

"Hurry up. I'm hungry and want to go home."

Liv scurried with her basket toward the other end of the store, her long purple dress flapping on her legs. She tugged on the thin ribbons of her white prayer *kapp* to make sure it wasn't crooked and almost ran in to her neighbor, Isaac Troyer.

She halted so fast, her basket tipped and her groceries clattered to the floor. "Hi, Isaac. I'm so sorry! I almost ran you over."

"It's all right, Liv. Don't worry about it!" He grinned, green eyes sparkling reassuringly. Then the smile slid from his face and concern shadowed his expression.

Fear swelled within her. Did he know?

She squirmed and avoided his gaze. "I'm so clumsy. I really should watch where I'm going." She shook her head, clearing her thoughts as she dropped to the floor to pick up her groceries. Isaac hurried to help her.

"Really, everyone does these things. So how are you, Liv?" he asked in all seriousness, using the nickname he used to call her when they had dated as teens. They had been so in love back then—until Jake came along and stole her heart with his cheap lies. Isaac was an old friend now and nothing more. The piece of her she had given to him when they had dated died the day she married Jake.

She told herself to act normal, even if he did suspect something. "I'm well. How are you?" She reached for a fallen box of cereal. Her purple sleeve rode up her arm, revealing a dark bruise. She took in a quick, sharp breath and yanked her sleeve down, turning away in shame.

Had he seen it?

Isaac rested his fingers on her arm. "Liv, be honest. Is Jake hurting you? Or did you 'walk into a door' again? You know I don't believe that nonsense. I've known Jake since we were children, and I know how angry he can get. And I know you might be silly sometimes, but you aren't that clumsy."

She sure wasn't silly anymore. Her silliness had also died the day she married Jake.

Olivia stared at Isaac wide-eyed, unable to breathe. He *did* know the truth about Jake. Her pulse quickened as the grocery store seemed to shrink around her, closing her in. Who else knew?

"You don't deserve this, Liv."

What would Jake do to her if he found out Isaac knew?

"Isaac…promise me you won't say anything. If you do, he will hurt me terribly. Maybe even—"

"Olivia! Are you okay?" Jake strode over to them. He helped her up in what seemed like a loving way, and no one else noticed his clenching grip on her arm.

Except Isaac. His eyes grew cold as his jaw tightened.

He knew.

Oh, God, please don't let him say anything.

No one would believe him even if he did. Jake was known for being a polite, helpful person. He was the kind of man who would help anyone at any time, even in the middle of the night or in a storm. No one would ever suspect him of hitting his wife.

He hid that side of himself skillfully, with his mask of deceptive charm that had made her fall in love with him so quickly.

Jake finished piling the groceries into the basket as Isaac stood.

"Good to see you, Isaac." Jake nodded to his former childhood friend.

"Likewise. Take care." Isaac offered a big smile as though nothing had happened.

When Liv glanced over her shoulder at him as she and Jake walked away, Isaac stared back at her, concern lining every feature of his face.

Most of the buggy ride home was nerve-wracking silence. They passed the green fields of summertime in Unity, Maine. Horses and cows grazed in the sunlight and Amish children played in the front yards. Normally she would have enjoyed watching them, but Olivia squeezed her eyes shut. She mentally braced herself for whatever storm raged in Jake's mind that he would soon unleash onto her.

"Want to tell me what happened back there?"

Jake's voice was not loud, but she could tell by his tone that he was infuriated. Who knew what awaited her at home?

"I bumped into Isaac and spilled my groceries. He was just helping me pick them up," she answered in a cool, calm voice. She clasped her hands together in her lap to stop them from shaking, acting as though everything was fine. Their buggy jostled along the side of the road as cars passed.

Did he know what had really happened?

"I was watching from a distance. I saw him touch your arm. I saw the way he smiled at you. And I saw the way you stared at him. You never look at me like that."

Here we go. She sucked in a deep breath, preparing for battle. At least he hadn't heard what Isaac had asked her. Jake was always accusing her of being interested in other men, but it was never true. He was paranoid and insecure.

"You know I love you, Jake."

"I know. But did you ever truly let go of Isaac before you married me? Does part of you still miss him?"

"No, of course not! You have all my love."

"Then why don't you act like it?" His knuckles turned white as he clenched his fists tighter around the reins. "Why don't you ever look at me like that?"

How could he expect her to shower him with love? She tried, but it was so hard to endure his rampages and live up to his impossible standards. Yes, she had married him and would stay true to her vows. She would remain by his side as his wife until death.

However soon that may be. Every time he had one of his rampages she feared for her life more and more.

She had given up on romance a long time ago. Now she just tried to survive.

If only her parents were still alive… but they had been killed along with the rest of her family in a fire when she had been a teenager. How many times had Liv wished that she could confide in her mother about Jake? She would have known what to do.

"I'm sorry, Jake. I'll try to do better." She told him what he wanted to hear.

"Good." Smugness covered his face as he glanced at her and sat up a bit taller.

When they arrived home, he helped her unload the groceries without saying a word. She knew what was coming. He internalized all his anger, and one small thing would send him over the edge once they were behind closed doors.

When everything was put away, he stalked off to the living room to wait as she prepared dinner. She began chopping vegetables, and not even ten minutes had passed when he stomped into the kitchen. As he startled her, the knife fell on the counter top.

Jake snarled through clenched teeth, crossing the room in three long strides. "You love him, don't you?"

"No, Jake! I told you I don't love him. I love you." She struggled to keep her voice steady. They had had this fight more than once.

"Are you secretly seeing each other?"

She spun around to face him. "No! I would never do that." She might wonder sometimes what her life would have been like if she had married Isaac, but that didn't mean she loved him or had feelings for him, and it certainly didn't mean she would have an affair with him. Happy or not, she was a married Amish woman and would never be unfaithful to her husband.

"I can see it all over your face. It's true. You are seeing him." He lunged toward her, pinning her against the counter top.

She tried to shield her face with her hands. The familiar feeling of overwhelming panic filled her. Her heart pounded as she anticipated what was coming. "No, that's not true!"

"After everything I've given you!" His eyes burned with an angry fire stronger than she had ever seen before. He raised his clenched fist and swung.

Pain exploded in her skull. Her head snapped back from the impact. Before she could recover, he wrapped his hands around her neck, squeezing harder and harder until her feet lifted off the floor.

She clawed at his hands, but he only clenched tighter. Her lungs and throat burned, her body screamed for oxygen.

This was it. She was going to die. She was sure of it.

A strange calm settled over her, and her eyes fluttered shut. It was better this way.

Her eyes snapped open.

No. Not today. For the first time in her life, she had to fight back.

She tried to punch him, but it was as if he didn't feel a thing. She tried to scream for help, but her vocal chords were being crushed. She reached behind her for anything to hit him in the head with. Her fingers fumbled with something sharp, and it cut her hand. But she ignored the pain.

The knife.

She gripped the handle. Before she could reconsider, she thrust the knife as hard as she could into the side of his neck.

Blood spurted from the wound as his grip loosened. His eyes widened in shock, and his knees gave out as he crumpled to the floor.

"What have I done?" She inhaled shaky breaths, struggling to get air back into her lungs. Tears stung her eyes. Bile crept up her throat, and she clamped a hand over her mouth. Panic and fear washed over her and settled in her gut.

She had stabbed her own husband.

A sob shook her chest. "Oh, dear Lord! Please be with me."

There was so much blood. Her stomach churned and her ears rang. Her head was weightless, and her vision tunneled into blackness. She slid against the handmade wooden cabinets to sit on the floor.

She should run to the phone shanty and call an ambulance, but she couldn't move. There was no way she could run or even walk all the way to the shanty without passing out. She would have gone next door to her aunt and uncle's house, but they were out of town.

As her vision tunneled, she wasn't sure if she was possibly losing consciousness or dying from being choked.

Either way, she was free.

Chapter Two

Six years later

"Jefferson! Run the other way!" Olivia shouted as she sprinted around the side of a broken-down house in Augusta, Maine. Her partner, Officer Jefferson Martin, bolted around the opposite side of the house, hoping to catch the culprit, who had just run to the other side. Maybe they could meet him in the middle and the criminal would be trapped in the fenced-in yard.

When Olivia thought of the young girl this man had kidnapped, she pushed herself even faster, her hair flying behind her. She reached the corner of the house, lifted her pistol, and swept the area. The perpetrator swung a rusty crowbar at her head. She ducked just in time to dodge it.

It thudded into the house right beside her face. She whipped around and shoved him up against the wall. "Nice try."

He struggled in her grasp, but she held onto him tightly as her partner rounded the corner and helped hold him down. When the perp would not stop wriggling and shouting protests, Jefferson pinned him to the ground and handcuffed him. "George Burke, you are under arrest for kidnapping. You have the right to remain silent…"

Jefferson finished reciting Burke's rights to him as he led him to the police car and shut the criminal inside. Jefferson questioned him about where the girl was, but the man said nothing.

"You think the girl is in there?" Olivia asked her partner, nodding toward the shabby house.

"Maybe, since he bolted out the back door when we pulled in the driveway. Let's go check it out."

A second patrol car arrived as backup and guarded the criminal while Olivia and Jefferson entered the house, weapons drawn.

"Not exactly a home fit for being in an interior decorating magazine." Olivia wrinkled her nose at the piles of dirty dishes in the kitchen, the messy floors, the questionable smells. In the laundry room, baskets of clothes covered the top of the washing machine. She held up her Military and Police Shield pistol as she poked her head around the corner. "Clear!"

"Clear in the living room!" Jefferson called.

"Let's check the basement."

They approached the door, and he quickly pulled it open. "Anybody down there? Police!"

No response. The partners glanced at each other, nodded, and descended the stairs, looking carefully for any sign of life or movement.

They poked around for about ten minutes, looking for some clue where they could find Miranda Nelson, the little girl Burke had kidnapped. They had evidence he had taken her, but they didn't know where he was keeping her.

"Hey, wasn't there a washing machine upstairs?" Olivia raised an eyebrow at the beat-up appliance placed crookedly against a wall.

"Yeah, there was."

"This one is just taking up space. I know this guy isn't very tidy, but why have two washing machines, especially when one looks like that? This might be nothing, but I have a weird feeling about it." Liv walked over to it and looked behind it. "There's something back here."

Jefferson hurried over and helped her move it aside to reveal a small door in the floor. Olivia reached down and flung it open. "Miranda? We're the police. Are you down there?" She reached for the flashlight on her belt.

A soft whimper sounded in the darkness. While Jefferson called the paramedics, Olivia aimed the beam of the flashlight in the hole in the floor, which revealed a space a little bigger than a small closet. There, illuminated by the light, sat a young girl with her hands tied and her mouth covered with duct tape.

Anger flooded Liv's veins. How could a person do this to a little girl? She had been missing for days. Who knew how long she had been down here? If only Olivia could get her hands on that guy...but she wouldn't. Besides, the other inmates in prison would show him how people felt toward criminals who kidnapped little children.

"Miranda, my name is Detective Olivia Mast, and I'm from a unit called Covert Police Detectives Unit. May I come down? This is my partner, Officer Jefferson Martin, and we are going to take you home."

The girl looked up at them for a moment with tired eyes, then slowly nodded.

Olivia climbed down, and Jefferson followed.

The girl began to make sounds, as if she was protesting. She couldn't speak with that tape over her mouth. What was she trying to tell them?

"Jefferson, go back up. I think she is afraid of men right now," Liv told him quietly.

"You go ahead." He climbed up and took a few steps away.

Olivia bent down and crawled to the girl in the small space. "I'm going to take those ropes off, okay? I'm going to cut them, but I'll be very careful."

The child calmed down and let Olivia saw through the knots with her pocket knife. "I'm going to take off the tape now."

After Liv pulled off the tape, Miranda winced but quickly recovered. "Are you really taking me home?" Her eyes grew big, hopeful.

"Yes, Miranda. Your family is waiting to see you. They missed you so much." Liv offered her hand. The girl's small hand held on, and Liv pulled her up. The child wobbled and fell into Liv's arms.

"My foot hurts. I can't walk." Miranda pointed to her ankle. Olivia wasn't sure if it was a sprain or not, but paramedics would be waiting outside soon.

"May I carry you, Miranda?" Olivia asked the girl.

Miranda nodded and reached up towards her. Olivia scooped her up and went back upstairs with Jefferson, who made sure the way was clear before them.

When they stepped outside, Miranda covered her eyes to shield them from the bright light. She probably hadn't seen the sun for several days. Olivia handed her to the paramedics so they could examine her.

"Stay here with me, Olivia." Miranda's voice sounded soft but desperate.

"Okay. I will."

"You did it again, Liv."

Liv turned to see Jefferson smiling at her. Her partner was a few years older than she was, around thirty, and handsome. She knew he liked her, but Olivia wanted to keep things professional. Besides, she was too devoted to her career to have time for a boyfriend.

"I'm impressed with how you found those clues that led us to the kidnapper. How did you know about the washing machine? And how did you know she didn't want me to come with you when you got her out?"

"If I were a little girl kidnapped by a man, I think I'd be afraid of men I don't know. Even a police officer."

"Well, it's a good thing we have female police officers, especially you. Victims trust you more, and you have a way with kids." He smiled at her again. "When you talk to kids, you're actually nice to them."

"What are you saying?" She playfully hit his arm. Liv didn't trust anyone, and she liked to be upfront with people, even if it wasn't polite. She was not the same meek and quiet woman who had left the Amish.

"You're not always as sweet as sugar, that's all." He gave her a nod. "I still can't believe you cut all your hair off. It looks great."

She tried not to blush as she reached up for the ends of her hair. "Thank you." She had recently cut her long, dark brown locks and now had a bob haircut with bangs. It had caramel highlights and was longer in the front, since the hairdresser had said that was in style. Liv hadn't really cared. She had just wanted it shorter.

Liv had grown up with long hair and had never been allowed to cut it. For a few years after she left her Amish community, it was hard for her to let go of. But finally she decided she needed a change, and she liked it. It was much better than the long French braid she had always worn it in, which always got in the way when she worked.

It had been her last tie to her Amish roots. She had even changed her last name from Sullivan back to her maiden name, Mast. Now that she didn't look Amish at all anymore, she could fully move on. Well, except for her Amish dress and prayer *kapp* in a box on the top shelf of her closet. She'd never be able to part with them because her mother had sewn them for her.

"So I hear you've got some vacation time saved up. You going to go anywhere?" Jefferson asked.

"I was thinking somewhere without snow. Maybe the Bahamas."

"You deserve it, Liv."

She didn't know about that, but she sure couldn't wait to get out of Maine for a while, away from all the heinous things she saw every day. She imagined a sparkling ocean with soft sand between her toes. And no one shooting at her.

Some commotion drew her attention, and she turned to see Miranda's father, Mr. Nelson, approaching and asking lots of questions. Olivia and Jefferson walked toward him.

"Hi, I'm Officer Jefferson Martin from Covert Police Detectives Unit. Detective Mast and I found your daughter today." Jefferson extended his hand.

"I just got to see Miranda, but I wanted to quickly thank the team for finding her. Where is this Detective Mast? I'd like to thank him personally." Mr. Nelson shook Jefferson's hand.

She cleared her throat. "I'm Detective Mast, sir." She stuck out her hand.

Mr. Nelson ignored her hand and stuck his hands in his pockets. "Oh. You're a detective? Really?" He gave her a once over.

Olivia tamped down her annoyance and crossed her arms. This was not the first time she had seen someone react like this. "Yes."

"She's the one who coaxed Miranda out of the house. Miranda wouldn't come near me. It's a good thing we have great detectives like Liv." Jefferson gave her a proud smile. That was one thing she loved about him. He always had her back in any situation. "In fact, Detective Mast found most of the clues today that led us to your daughter. She was the one who discovered where she was being kept, in a secret room under a washing machine."

"Is that so?" Mr. Nelson looked her over again. "You don't really look like a cop. You're too pretty to be a detective." He flashed her a smile, and Jefferson raised one eyebrow. She wanted to roll her eyes.

Ugh.

"Well, nice to meet you. I need to go check on Miranda." She spun on her heel and marched back toward the medical team. The girl tugged on her sleeve and stared at her, even smiling a little.

"I prayed God would send an angel to rescue me," she said in a soft voice.

Olivia couldn't help but chuckle. "I'm no angel, kid."

"But God did send you. Thank you for coming to get me," she replied as the paramedic inspected her ankle.

"You're welcome, Miranda."

Liv hadn't prayed in six years, and she didn't plan on doing so anytime soon.

She had left God behind the day she had left the Amish.

*

"Olivia, come see me in my office." Captain Branson took a swig of his coffee and nodded his balding head toward his office door at Covert Police Detectives Unit headquarters in Portland, Maine. Bodyguards, police officers, special agents, and detectives all worked together in this building and in the field. Liv loved this place.

"In a minute. I'm just—"

"Now, Liv!" he shouted and disappeared into the office.

With a sigh, she closed the vacation website on her laptop and put the gorgeous images of the Bahamas out of her mind. She finally got a minute to herself at her desk, and *now* Branson wanted to talk. She picked herself up and stepped into his office, wondering what she had done wrong. Had she forgotten to label evidence or wipe out the microwave in the break room? Or was it the prank she played on Jefferson last week?

Man, she had gotten him good.

"Have a seat."

It had to have been the prank. Maybe putting a fake snake in his car had been too much.

"What's up, Captain?" She plopped into one of his chairs. A feeling of dread began to creep over her. Maybe she actually was in trouble.

He settled in his chair and pulled it forward, his round belly pressed up against the desk. "I have an undercover assignment for you."

At least she wasn't in trouble.

"Captain, with all due respect, you know I was planning on going on a vacation soon."

"Liv, I need you for this one. No one else will do." He adjusted his glasses and handed her pictures of a crime scene. "Bill Sullivan was shot and killed in his barn last night in Unity, Maine. He was an Amish man in his fifties. Someone outside the community reported this."

Shock ricocheted throughout her system. A crime in Unity? Her heart sank, even if she had never really liked the man much. "I knew this man when I lived there. He was my father-in-law."

"I'm sorry," Branson said.

"We weren't exactly chummy, but still…" She stared at the photos in disbelief, dozens of questions spiraling in her head. Liv had never witnessed any violence in her community except for her husband's abuse and the arsonist who had killed her family. Usually Amish communities were peaceful, but sometimes criminals or rowdy teenagers liked to take advantage of the fact that the Amish didn't report crimes like vandalism or arson…or murder.

Was the rest of the community all right? Had anyone else been injured?

Wait…*no!*

"You want me to go there, don't you?" She was ready to argue her way out of this one. She slammed her palms down on his desk as she stood. "You know I never want to go there ever again."

"Liv, calm down. I know it's against the Amish way to give police any information. But we need to find this killer, and you grew up Amish. If I send any of my other detectives there, they'll stand right out. Besides, they don't know anything about the Amish, and they won't be able to blend in unnoticed. I need you to go there and act like you're one of them again. The killer won't even know the crime was reported or that we are onto him. Can't you just ask to rejoin the church?"

"It's really not that simple." She crossed her arms, looked away, and plopped back down in her chair.

"Why not? Just tell them you want to come back like old times."

"I'm shunned. When people leave, they are shunned. That means no one will speak a word to me unless I repent before the church, beg for forgiveness, and act like I sincerely want to become Amish again." She shuddered at the thought.

"Then do it. Whatever it takes. Since the community in Unity won't accept the help of the police or answer our questions, we think the only way to help these people is for you to go there covertly and investigate without them even knowing it. And the killer will have no idea. No one from their community even reported this crime or planned to. An outsider found out through some gossip and reported it. One of the customers of the community store."

"I know they don't ask the police for help. They believe everything is God's will, and they leave the vengeance to Him. I'm just not sure they'll welcome me back as easily as you think they will."

"Come on. Aren't they nice, forgiving people?"

"They are, but..." She shut her eyes and saw the flames engulfing her home with her parents and siblings dying inside. The arsonist was never found. The elders had told her not to report the crime or look for the man who had murdered her family because their way was to forgive and move on.

But she had held on to the bitterness. She couldn't forgive the killer.

And now she had to go back there? To the place where her family had been killed and her husband had abused her?

Her heart clenched at the thought of returning to her hometown. She hadn't been there in six years. And she had not left on good terms. It wouldn't be as easy as Branson thought it would be. She couldn't just waltz into the community and ask to be forgiven for leaving, could she?

And for killing Jake in self-defense? She didn't think so. All those memories would come rushing back, and it would be too much to deal with. Bile rose in her throat at the thought of returning.

"I can't do this, Captain. I'll do anything else. Send me on a dangerous mission. I don't care. Just don't make me do this. Please." She leaned forward in her chair, put her nice face on, and pleaded with wide-open eyes. "I'd rather run through gunfire than go back there. I'd rather die."

Branson shook his head firmly. "Don't be so dramatic, Liv. If you want your vacation time—if you want your job—you have to do this."

"My job?" A feeling of dread and panic settled over her. Her job was everything to her. She had no life outside of work.

"Look, Liv. Our funds have been reduced, and we have been forced to make cuts. You're a great detective, but you're one of the newer ones. Some of our people have been here ten or fifteen years or more. The board would probably pick you as the first to go if we have to lay people off. So if you do this mission and prove yourself worthy, you would make them reconsider."

She'd rather rot in jail than go back there. She scowled.

"Olivia. I need you to do this."

She gave him a sideways look.

"I'll give you an extra week of vacation time if you go tomorrow and stay until this killer is caught."

"Seriously?" Her eyebrows rose as her interest piqued.

"Don't you go telling anyone. Consider it a bonus for a job well done. I don't know much about what your history is with that place. I'm sorry if this is personal, but don't let it be. Just do your job, and you'll be on the beach sipping a margarita before you know it."

"I don't drink."

"Whatever. Just imagine this—two weeks in the Bahamas, and you don't have to talk to me the entire time."

She nodded slowly, smiling. Sounded like paradise. "How'd you know I want to go there?"

"I've got ears everywhere." He chuckled and leaned back in his chair.

Jefferson must have talked to him.

"Okay, fine. If it will help save lives and catch the killer, I'll do it."

"One more thing. Isaac Troyer, a thirty-year-old Amish man, was also attacked last night. Blunt force trauma to the head. He had traces of wood in his wounds, which were from whatever he was rendered unconscious with." He slid another photo toward her.

Isaac? Her mind screamed at the image of the man she had once loved. She jumped back from the photo as if she had been burned on a hot wood stove.

"He was then left on one of the lanes in the community near his house until a Sid Hoffman brought him to the local hospital. Since this happened on the same night as the murder, we think he was possibly a witness to the crime. You need to covertly protect him, since the Amish won't accept police protection, and he could be the perp's next target. The thing is, Troyer has localized amnesia. He can't remember what happened the night he was assaulted, but keep asking him questions without being obvious. Once you take him home, he might remember more of what happened."

Could this get any worse? She had to take Isaac back to Unity and protect him? Him of all people?

How was she going to act normal around him, try to get information from him, and protect him during what would be the most awkward encounter of her entire life? She had asked him to run away with her and leave the church, but he had refused and broken her heart. Spontaneous butterflies erupted in her stomach at the thought of him, but she ignored them.

How would he react to her?

The last time she had seen him she had kissed him. Right after her husband had died. After that, he had testified on her behalf during her trial. The jury had acquitted her, finding she had acted in self-defense once they saw the evidence—her bruised neck and other injuries, some of which were older and had not properly healed. Because she had left the church after Jake's death, she had reported what had happened to the police herself, knowing she'd be found innocent.

After the verdict, she hadn't had the courage to speak to him. All she had been able to do was give him a small smile, silently thanking him for testifying before a swarm of news reporters surrounded her, all wanting more details about the Amish woman who had killed her husband in self-defense.

"What's the matter? You know him too?" Branson asked.

"Yeah, I do."

"Are you okay?"

"Yes, Captain."

"You sure? Anything I should know about?"

"I dated him a long time ago when I was a teenager. That's all."

"Okay, that actually works in our favor. Since he is a potential witness, we need you to go talk to him. If he is still single, rekindle your relationship with him—whatever it was you shared—and drive him back home. The closer you get, the better. Stick to him like glue. If he is a witness, he needs your protection."

Like glue? Really? She let her head drop in her hands dramatically.

"Okay, Liv?" Branson prodded, leaning forward and slightly raising his voice.

"Okay." She sighed heavily.

The Bahamas would have to wait.

"Hey, this is none of my business either, but I know a little bit of what happened there, how you killed your husband in self-defense."

"Yeah. I did."

"Why? What did he do? If I may ask."

Could he get any nosier?

"After abusing me for three years, he tried to choke me to death, so I stabbed him," Olivia said emotionlessly. "I had no choice. The community didn't report it. I did, because I knew I was innocent. And the jury and judge agreed once they saw the evidence and heard the testimonies." She stood up and walked out of the office, leaving her boss wide-eyed.

Chapter Three

After work, Olivia drove home to her small white house on a street lined with similar houses in Augusta. It was in a part of the city that was complete with quaint parks, but she never took advantage of them. She preferred to give her life over to her job, to help the victims of horrific crimes. It was the only thing that made her forget her past.

She pounded the steering wheel in frustration. The last thing she wanted to do was put on her old Amish clothing, which she had avoided looking at since she had moved here, and go see the man she had loved before she was married.

A long time ago, Liv had convinced herself that they had never loved each other. That it had just been a summer infatuation. Teenage puppy love. Nothing real.

But her heart said her head was lying. Especially when she had kissed him the day she had left Unity.

The heart said all kinds of foolish things. How many times she had questioned criminals and victims alike who had just been "following their hearts"?

She didn't trust what her own heart had to say. When she had left the faith, she had vowed to make decisions based on logic, not emotions.

Isaac had probably forgotten all about her years ago and had most likely married some sensible woman by now. He probably even had a few kids.

Her stomach churned at the thought.

Get it together, Liv. She pulled into her narrow driveway. Isaac's personal life was none of her business. She had to get dressed, head over to the hospital, and somehow convince Isaac and the entire community that she wanted to be Amish again.

She laughed aloud at the thought. She would rather die than rejoin their church. But this would all be for her cover. It wasn't real.

Forgiveness was very important to the Amish, but would Aunt Mary, Uncle Gideon, and Maria be able to forgive her once they found out the truth? She'd be shunned again after this was over anyway, but she still hoped they would understand she was just doing her job.

There would be no turning back. But if that was the price she had to pay to keep the community safe and stop the killer, so be it.

She shut off her car and gathered her purse, cell phone, and keys. Before opening the door and stepping outside, she looked around for anyone nearby who could be a potential threat. A hooded man, a shadow... She had recently investigated a woman who had been murdered while getting out of her car. She briefly touched the edge of her M&P Shield in her holster, just to reassure herself the gun was still there, even though she knew it was. It made her feel safer.

Some would call her paranoid. She was just cautious.

Sometimes she swore someone was watching her, and sometimes she thought she saw a shadow moving outside or in her house. But it always ended up being nothing. No one was ever there.

Maybe she really was just paranoid.

She hurried up the short walkway, then let herself in and locked the door. Dropping her things onto a black wooden table near the door, she looked around her neat, modern house. Black wooden furniture, beige walls, splashes of red in the kitchen and blue in the living room. Her mother would never have approved of all the luxuries, appliances, and color. Though her mother had been very old-fashioned, Liv had loved her dearly, and she smiled at the thought of her.

Liv filled up a glass of cold water and drank it as she envisioned the dress packed away in a box high up in her closet. She dreaded taking it down and putting it on.

But she had to do it. Then, when this whole thing was over, she could keep her job and go to the Bahamas.

And she would forget about Unity. And Isaac. Again. All while sitting on the sandy shores of paradise.

Alone. As always.

Good plan. She double-checked that the deadbolt on the door was locked, then walked to her bedroom.

She wanted to procrastinate. Well, she *was* hungry. She decided to eat dinner, then get the dress. Satisfied with her decision, she went to the kitchen and heated up a microwavable meal of chicken alfredo from the freezer.

As she ate, she thought about what she would say to Isaac. Since his amnesia was only related to the night he was attacked, he would remember her. Would he believe her? Would he laugh at her?

Oh, gosh. What if he was still single?

She felt bad enough for abandoning him for the jerk she had

married. Knowing that there was still a possibility of them getting back together...

A small flame of hope sparked within her, then she shook her head. Who was she kidding?

She was an *Englisher*, an outsider who was not Amish. Isaac would never break the rules and knowingly start a romantic relationship with an outsider, and he would never leave the community. Besides, she never let emotions interfere with her job.

She was finally beginning to accept that she might be single for the rest of her life.

She practically threw her fork and cup in the sink, barely cringing at the crashing sound, and trudged over to her closet. She had to get this over with or it would make her crazy.

She tore open the door and yanked down the box before she changed her mind. After ripping off the lid, she slid the plain fabric between her fingers, fighting back tears. Longing swelled inside her, those feelings she had hidden just like this box of clothes for so many years.

Oh, how she missed her mother. Her father. Her siblings.

Life in Unity had been great when they were alive, but once they were gone, the grief of their deaths had consumed her.

Anger and sorrow welled up within her as the memories of the flames seeped into her mind. The fact that the arsonist had not been caught was one of the biggest reasons why she had become a detective.

She lifted up the white prayer *kapp* her mother had helped her stitch. Her mother used to laugh at her when she sewed. Olivia had always been terrible at sewing, cleaning, cooking, and all the things an Amish girl was supposed to excel at. Instead, as a child Olivia had usually been caught racing the boys outside, getting dirty or climbing trees.

She had never been the ideal Amish girl, but her family had adored her anyway.

Liv pulled out the dress, a lavender one with a black apron, and put it on.

Her mother had hand-sewn this only a few months before the fire. Liv ran her fingers over the impeccable stitching and willed her heart not to break all over again. This was what she had worn when she had sneaked out on the night of the fire. It was all she had left of her former life.

Recently she had been having fewer memories and flashbacks of Jake's outbursts and rampages. Fewer memories of her family's love. Even fewer memories of Isaac. Each day she thought of her old life less and less. Sometimes a whole day would pass and she would realize she had not thought of her past once all day.

And then this had to happen. Branson had to pick *her* to become buddy-buddy with the people who had shunned her for leaving.

And to protect the man she had once loved.

She squeezed her eyes shut. The beaches of the Bahamas would be worth it, right? She moved on with her task of dressing.

She let out an exasperated sigh. Where the heck was she supposed to conceal her .45 and be able to pull it out at a second's notice?

She felt around, looking for a flap in the dress or somewhere she could hide the weapon. She wouldn't be able to easily pull out a firearm without hiking her skirt up, which would be quite scandalous in Unity. But that was the way it was going to have to be.

She secured her M&P Shield on her leg and clipped her badge onto the leg holster. She really didn't like leg holsters much. Her normal holster was so much more accessible and comfortable. But it was only temporary.

Liv tried to pull her hair into a bun, which was hard to do since it was so short, so it ended up being a messy ponytail. She smoothed out the *kapp* and yanked it on, not bothering to tie it, and looked in her full-length mirror.

This was as Amish as she was going to look. Oh wait. She had to wipe off her makeup.

She washed her face, removing the mascara, eyeliner, and light brown eye shadow she had been wearing. She adjusted her *kapp* back into place.

Now she looked the part. She looked just as scared as she had the day she first approached her mother-in-law about Jake's cruelty. The same wide eyes, pale face, and racing heart.

Liv was nothing like the woman she had been the day she had gone to Diana's house to tell her about Jake. She had been hoping for Diana's help. Not rejection.

Diana had let her in and made her a pot of tea, then they sat down at the kitchen table. Bill had been at work, so it was just the two of them.

"How are you doing, Olivia?" Diana poured Liv a steaming cup of tea.

"That's why I'm here. I need to talk to you about Jake."

"What about?" Diana poured herself a cup and mixed in some honey.

Liv sucked in a shaky breath. "There's no easy way to say this. With my family gone, you are the only mother I have now, besides Aunt Mary. But you are Jake's mother, so I came to you first."

"What's wrong, love?" Diana leaned forward in concern. Gray tresses streaked throughout her brown hair that peeked through under her *kapp*.

Liv choked, unable to utter the words, "Jake hit me." Instead, she opened the back of her dress and showed Diana a large bruise on her upper back from when he had pushed her in to a bookshelf.

"What happened to you? Did you walk into a door again?"

"No. How would I get this from walking in to a door? Jake did this to me! He's been abusing me for three years. At first, I thought it was my fault. But I realize now no matter what I do, he'll keep abusing me. I can't live like this anymore. What should I do?" Liv began to cry. She pulled a tissue from her apron and dabbed her eyes. "With my family gone, I thought I should tell you first. I'm so sorry you had to find out like this."

Diana stared at her in disbelief. She blinked once, again. Then she stood up.

"That can't be true. I don't know what you're talking about. Are you making this up?"

"What?" Dismay flooded her veins. She felt her face go pale. This could not be happening.

"My son would never beat his wife." Diana tipped up her chin in defiance.

"Look at this!" Liv retorted, pointing to her back.

"I don't know where you got that, and I don't care. Even if Jake did hit you, sometimes I think you deserve it. You can't cook, you can't sew, and now you are making up lies about him. You haven't had any children yet. You're not a proper Amish woman. My son could have married any woman he wanted, but he chose you. You must understand and forgive him for being disappointed in you. But I do not believe he is capable of hurting you like that. There is no way he's abusing you."

Liv's heart plummeted to the hardwood floor. "You're saying you don't believe me?"

"That's right. I don't believe you."

Olivia saw anger in Diana's eyes, deep pain that had been concealed by good deeds and a smiling face for years. Was Diana hiding something too, like Liv had been?

Was her husband abusive, too? Bill Sullivan had not been born Amish. He had left his troubled past in the outside world and married into the community, but it seemed like he had never quite let go of the bitterness of his former life. Their youngest child, Ava, died in a drowning accident while her brothers were supposed to be watching her swim; maybe that had triggered Bill's violence.

The three Sullivan brothers—Ian, Samuel, and Jake—had all seemed like such happy and carefree children long ago, but they had become withdrawn after the accident. Jake especially was never the same.

Had Bill turned violent after Ava's death? Was this why Jake was so cruel and abusive, because of his father's abuse? Because it was all he knew? Even still, Jake should have broken the cycle of abuse. Liv had asked him about his father being abusive several times, but Jake never wanted to talk about it, which made Liv believe her suspicions were correct.

Even though he terrified her, Liv felt sorry for her husband for having to endure such a painful childhood.

Was Bill still taking his anger out on Diana?

Poor Diana, Liv thought. *She's living in the same situation as me, probably feeling just as afraid and trapped. Is she too scared to admit she knows I'm telling the truth?*

Diana's words sank in even more, and the pain of rejection crushed Liv, seeping into every pore of her body, which hurt worse than when Jake hit her.

"Get out," Diana seethed through clenched teeth. "And don't speak about my son in such a way again."

Olivia turned and reluctantly walked out, heart and soul heavy with sorrow, feeling as though her limbs weighed a hundred pounds each. She let the tears come, and she sobbed in the woods for an hour afterward.

But that was Olivia Sullivan back then—weak, defeated, and a pushover. The Olivia today, Olivia Mast, would have spoken her mind to Diana. She would have gone up to Jake and—

Well, she wasn't sure quite what, but she would have beat him at his own game, that was for sure.

Literally.

Chapter Four

Olivia parked her car in the hospital parking lot under gray clouds that blotted out the sun. The brick red building seemed to loom over her ominously, and she groaned.

"I can't do this." She rested her head on the steering wheel. She'd rather—

What? Lose her job?

No. She had to do this. Shutting off the car, she stuck her cell phone and keys in her purse, straightened her *kapp,* and made sure there was nothing stuck in her teeth. No need to make this meeting more awkward or embarrassing than it had to be.

Once in the lobby, she extracted her phone and checked her notes to see which room he was in. The elevator dinged, and she entered it. Her pulse pounded. She would so much rather be on a tropical beach right now.

When the door opened, she followed the signs to Isaac's room. Hopefully, he was asleep, and she could come back later. She tapped on the door.

"Come in."

Great. He was awake. *Don't let it be personal. Just do your job.*

Before she could think any more about it, she walked inside and stopped short. Poor Isaac. The last time she had seen him, she had been the one with the bruises, but now, he was the one with bruises and bandages on his head. A Bible lay open on his lap, the same worn Bible he had always carried around when they were young.

They stared at each other, and he raised his eyebrows. "Liv?"

Her throat tightened as he beckoned her into the room.

"Come in, Liv! What are you doing here? I mean, you still live in Maine?" The same low voice—so familiar, yet somehow so far away.

Liv ran her fingers over the impeccable stitching on the hem of her sleeve and willed her heart rate to slow down. She walked toward him and hesitantly sat in the chair next to him. "Yeah, I do. I heard you got hurt, so I came to see you." She choked out the words and faked a smile, pretending to not be affected by his closeness.

His face was shaved except for some stubble that shaded the edge of his square jaw. That meant he was unmarried...and maybe without a girlfriend.

Oh, God, please help me.

After all this time, of course Isaac Troyer would be the reason she prayed again.

"What have you been doing here? I mean, since you left?" he asked.

Good question. She hesitated, and guilt gripped her insides. "You know, just working at a local restaurant. I've been renting an apartment not far from here. I just decided to return home today. I wanted to come see you first." Lies, all lies. But she had a job to do.

"Ah. So that is why you are still carrying your phone."

She had forgotten to put it back in her purse. "Haven't gotten rid of all my *Englisher* things quite yet. But I will."

As if she would ever really get rid of her phone.

"Was it all you thought it would be? The *Englisher's* world?" His green eyes asked many more silent questions than the ones he voiced. Maybe he was wondering if she was with someone. She stared back at him, wishing she had eyelashes as long and dark as his.

"No. I want to come home. I want to rejoin the church." The worst lie of all.

"Oh, good!" He reached for her hand and squeezed it. "I have been praying you would return one day."

"Really?" Her heart melted. He had not forgotten her? Had he really thought of her often?

Stop! Focus.

"Yes, Liv. I've prayed for you every day since you left." He gave her hand another squeeze and rested his free hand on his Bible.

An overwhelming sense of admiration and gratitude struck her. He had been praying for *her?* She sucked in a deep breath. Was this really happening? Her eyes prickled with unshed tears that would have to wait. She blinked them away. "Enough about me. What happened to you?"

"I don't remember. I just remember waking up in this bed. Everyone tells me Sid Hoffman brought me here. Someone hit me in the head with something and knocked me out, and he found me after. I don't know what happened." He shrugged. "But all is well now."

"All is not well. Bill Sullivan was murdered." She then lowered her voice, trying to calm down. "Do you know anything about his death?"

"Liv, I know it was a terrible thing that happened, but we must leave vengeance to God," he said in his low, calming voice. "Do not worry about such things."

"You don't want to know who murdered Bill Sullivan?" Her voice rose again.

"No. God will take care of it."

As if a killer on the loose was no big deal. This was why she had left the church. It was their way to forgive and leave the rest to God, but she couldn't stand the thought of ignoring a crime.

"Why do you want to know so much about it?" he asked.

"If I am going to live in Unity again, I want to know whether it's safe."

"Right. I do see your point. Well, you don't have to worry. God will protect us if it's His will."

"I think once you return home you'll remember more of the accident." She tried to distract herself from her own depressing thoughts with the hope that he would recall the incident.

"Even if I did, I would not report the person who did this to me."

How could he say that? She took a deep breath and looked toward the window. "What if reporting it could save more lives? What if it prevented this person from hurting more people?"

"As I said, this is all in God's hands. If you will be rejoining us, you must accept these things."

She was not getting anywhere with him. "Hopefully you can go home soon. Do you want a ride home?"

"I'd appreciate it. You haven't officially rejoined the church yet, so thankfully, you can still drive. Then we won't have to hire a driver. Are you going to get rid of your car once you move back home?"

Uh oh. She hadn't thought of that. Maybe Jefferson or one of the guys could come get it. Or she could hide it in the woods somewhere, like some of the teenage boys did when they bought trucks on their *Rumspringa.*

"Yeah. I guess I'll sell it."

"Everyone will be so glad to have you back." He reached for her hand again.

His touch sent sparks up her arm. Why did he still have this effect on her? It had been years since they had been together. Why couldn't her heart rate slow down just a little bit? She wasn't a teenager anymore.

"Are you sure they'll welcome me back? I mean, I killed Jake, even though it was self-defense."

"Right. It was self-defense. The police, the jury, and the court decided that when you went to court. And God would also agree. Once you ask for forgiveness, the community will accept you immediately."

He looked into her eyes, and she couldn't look away. He had some type of invisible, magnetic, almost magical hold on her, as if he could control her like a marionette doll. And he had no idea.

Her heart didn't mind at all, but her police-trained brain told her she was being foolish.

"You really think so?" The community and the church might welcome her back, but Jake's mother and brother, Diana and Samuel Sullivan, might not. They certainly weren't like the rest. Their family had always been different because Bill Sullivan had grown up *Englisher* and married into the Amish, bringing all his baggage with him.

"Of course. The community will be glad to have you back."

Why did he have to be so charming and boyish? This was going to be the hardest undercover mission she had ever done.

Chapter Five

Finally, the snow was melting. Hopefully, they wouldn't see snow again for a long time. Winters in Maine always seemed to last forever, and it was not unusual to get a snowfall in March or April.

"You look better today." Olivia wheeled Isaac out of the hospital in a wheelchair. "Not that you didn't look good yesterday."

He grinned and looked up at her, catching her blushing, and chuckled at her awkwardness. Then he changed the subject. "Do you really need to push me in this thing?"

"Yes. Would you relax? Now wait here while I go get my car, okay?"

Isaac nodded, still smiling as he watched Liv walk to her car.

He would not lie to himself about one thing—she looked great. She didn't look a day older than when she had left Unity. That dress still fit her the same as it had in her early twenties, though she did look stronger and more nourished, and she still had the same beautiful smile. However, he had quickly realized her change of attitude.

But that was not strange to him. He had known her as a carefree, awkward, spunky teenager and had loved her then. Then he watched her turn into a withdrawn, pensive, fearful woman after she had married his friend, Jake. The brave and strong side of her came alive the day Jake died. She had changed so much before she had left the faith, and he loved every facet of her. He hadn't quite figured out this new Liv yet, but he could tell she was strong, opinionated, stubborn, and independent now.

Not quite Amish material, but he liked this side of Liv just as much as the other sides of her personality. Every color of her spirit and character fascinated him. She was like a kaleidoscope—always changing, always vivid, always surprising.

When she pulled up to the hospital entrance, he chuckled again. Her driving a car while dressed in her Amish garb was so funny-looking. She had also driven on her *Rumspringa*, though she had never participated in drinking, drugs, or partying. And neither had he. Though she had never done anything immoral, she had fun during that short time when Amish youths experience the outside world. At least she had been given a chance to live freely before she had married Jake.

But Jake was gone. And right now, it was just Isaac and Liv.

He knew he should feel guilty, caring for his deceased friend's widow in such a way. But he didn't. Not after the way Jake treated her. Jake had never deserved her. Had never loved her. And even though they had grown up together, clearly Isaac had not known Jake as well as he thought.

What if I had married her? He wondered it for the millionth time. But he pushed the thought out of his head. He couldn't think like that. The *what ifs* could make a man crazy.

Liv stepped out of the car. "Need help?"

"No, no. I'm fine." Isaac stood up and started towards the car, but then a wave of dizziness struck him. He groaned and fell into his wheelchair. "I'm okay," he mumbled, touching his head. Liv rushed to his side. "Just as stubborn as you used to be. You haven't changed much. Come on."

She offered him her hand and he took it, resting his large arm on her smooth, fair skin. For a moment, he was afraid of leaning on her too much. Then he remembered this woman was the strongest person he had ever met. She had already been through so much.

"You're one to talk." He wanted to rest his other hand on her arm, just to feel the softness of her skin even more, but he held back, letting her support him as he stumbled into the car. She helped him get situated.

"All set?" She smiled.

"Yes. *Danki.*"

"You're welcome." Her smile faded a little at his Pennsylvania Dutch as she turned away to return the wheelchair. Why had that upset her? Once she returned to Unity, they would be speaking a lot more of that form of German. It was the language spoken more often than English in their community; the children didn't even learn English until they went to school.

She strode to the driver's side, got in, and slammed the door shut, glancing at him. The smile was back, though not as strong. "Let's roll." She revved the engine then started driving.

He couldn't help but wonder how she was truly feeling about returning home.

"You're oddly quiet. You okay?" Isaac asked after they had been driving in the car for a while. Liv had barely said a word.

"Oh, yeah. I'm fine." She had taken off her *kapp*, probably so she could see the road better. She had always complained about wearing it. She flipped it out of her eyes.

He was a little surprised to see the ends of her hair just brushing her shoulders. Her bangs hid her eyes from him, so he could stare at her without her knowing it. The sunlight shone on the golden streaks in her chocolate-colored strands, and it looked so soft, he wished he could run his hands through it like he had when they had dated.

This was not the first time he had seen her with her *kapp* off. They had both known that a woman's hair was only meant to be seen by her husband and family, but Liv had always been a bit rebellious. She had removed her *kapp* many times around him. Back then, her hair had been so long it had almost reached her knees, just like his mother's and sisters', but Liv's hair had always been so much more fascinating and beautiful to him. It was so different now—lighter and shorter—and he loved it.

She drummed the steering wheel with her fingers and tapped her foot, even though there was no music playing.

"You're nervous," he observed.

"I am not!" she shot back, making a left turn.

He scratched his head and rolled it to the right, looking out the window at the edge of the endless freeway.

"I'd be nervous," he offered. In the corner of his eye, he saw her glance at him.

"I mean, yeah, I'm a little worried about how everyone will react to seeing me. I mean, I killed Jake."

He couldn't stop himself from reaching over and giving her wrist a gentle squeeze. "Let's pray they have found the strength to forget all that and welcome you back."

She opened her mouth to say something, possibly an argument, then bit her lip. She let out a deep breath. "You're right."

"We're almost there."

"I know. I remember the way," she murmured, a far-off look in her eyes.

Had she come back over the past few years, hoping to return, but chickened out at the last moment? He didn't feel right asking her. Maybe this place was just hard to forget.

They passed the old *Welcome to Unity* sign, along with a yellow street sign with a horse and buggy on it. They passed a café and a pizza place that his family sometimes went to, then the modern world slowly faded away as they drove on.

Besides the buggy sign, there was no sign announcing that Amish lived there. Besides an occasional horse and buggy going down the road or a few Amish walking by in their old-fashioned clothing, it was not obvious to a passerby that this was an Amish community. The houses weren't that different, besides the lack of power lines and window shutters, and the farms did not particularly stand out. The road that passed the community had a fast speed limit, so cars whizzed by every day, and sometimes Isaac wondered if the drivers even noticed the community or the serenity that always surrounded the Amish lifestyle.

Then he realized Liv's hands trembled.

He didn't know what to say, so he said nothing. He couldn't even imagine what she must be feeling.

*

Liv had no problem running through gunfire to chase a criminal. She was not afraid of wrestling a perp to the ground, nor would she hesitate before putting her life at risk to rescue a victim. But her old home and all the bad memories associated with it made her heart pound and her palms sweat.

She really did not want to take a trip down memory lane.

A deep breath helped calm her as she pictured a clear ocean, white sands, wind in her hair, warm sunlight. No cold weather or snow.

This would be so worth it once she arrested the killer. Her pistol bumped against her leg, and she was calmed by the security of its protection. She took a deep breath. Today, all she would have to do was see her aunt and uncle. She had moved in with them after she became orphaned by the fire. They were like her second parents.

Well, they had been before she had left. She must have devastated them, but it was something she had had to do, and she hoped they had understood.

Memories from the day she had left came washing over her as she drove closer to their destination. She let her mind wander back to the day she had left her community.

Jake had attacked her and accused her of loving Isaac. His blood had encircled his body on the floor after she had stabbed him.

Jake had never loved her.

Olivia had sat on the kitchen floor for several minutes after Jake died, just trying to take in what had just happened.

He was dead.

She had killed her husband. What was going to happen? Would she go to prison?

Olivia sat there, sobbing and shaking. She drew in several deep breaths, trying to lower her heart rate, and tried not to look at Jake. There was so much blood.

She had to do something. Maybe she should leave. Where would she go? She didn't know much about the outside world, only what she had experienced during the short time she had spent trying it out in her *Rumspringa*. She didn't know how to actually live in the outside world and do things like get a job, pay an electric bill, or find an apartment. How would she survive?

All she knew was she did not belong here anymore, and she would rather die out there than continue living a lie here. Would anyone believe her, that it had been self-defense? She had never told anyone about Jake's abuse except for Diana, who hadn't believed her, and her aunt and uncle. After Diana's reaction, she had been too afraid to tell anyone else, afraid the community wouldn't believe her and that Jake would find out and hurt her more violently than he ever had.

Or even kill her. Which he had tried to do anyway.

Her relatives were out of town. Who could she tell? She had to talk to someone.

Isaac. He was the only other person who knew about Jake and would help her. He would know what to do, and he was right down the lane.

Once her stomach finally stopped churning and her head stopped spinning, she picked herself up and left the house. She didn't have a plan, but she hoped he could help her figure out what to do.

She pounded on his door. "Isaac? Are you home?"

A moment later he answered her knock, and his face almost turned white. "What happened to you? Did he hurt you?" He pulled her inside before she could even answer. "You're covered in blood. What did he do to you? If I ever get my hands on that guy—" Isaac's fists balled up. A vein protruded from his neck.

Liv's eyes filled with tears, and a lump grew in her throat. "He's dead!"

"What? How?"

"I stabbed him. He was trying to kill me," she managed to say between sobs.

Isaac reached out and gently touched her marred neck. "Did he try to choke you?" His voice was soft, and he let his hand rest on her shoulder. He looked her in the eyes.

She nodded, unable to speak. His touch brought back old feelings of the love they used to share. He took her in his arms and held her close, and she drew in a sharp breath. She was pressed up against his tall, wide frame, and all the memories of when they had dated came flooding back. For the first time since her family had died, she felt safe.

She had loved him when they had dated. Truly loved him. And she had thrown it all away for an angry man who had never loved her at all.

She would always regret that.

"I knew he was hurting you. I should have done something," he said in a low voice.

"This is not your fault. It's mine."

"It is not your fault at all!" He pulled away and stared at her. "None of this is your fault." He reached up and tenderly stroked her cheek where a bruise was forming. "I should have asked you to marry me. I was planning on asking you when we were dating, you know. I would have loved you unconditionally. I would have taken good care of you. I never understood why you married him."

His words must have spilled out before he had had the chance to think about what he was going to say, because he blushed a deep red. "I'm so sorry. That was out of line." He let go of her and stepped back, looking at the floor.

"It's okay. I married Jake because he was charming. He convinced me he was head over heels in love with me. He made me believe that what you and I shared was teenage puppy love. He promised me a fairy tale future. It was a whirlwind of romance and fake promises. And then we were at the church getting married. It all happened so fast." Before she could think twice, she said, "And you're right. I know you would have loved me if you had married me." As she dared to look up at his face, his expression made her smile. In his eyes she saw how much he cared about her.

She desperately wanted to know what it felt like to be loved again. The day's events had tampered with her brain, and it had stopped working properly. Her heart took over. Her foolish heart that had led her to this—covered in blood and bruises, a widow seeking help from

Isaac Troyer.

She grabbed onto his suspenders, pulled him towards her, reached up to hold on to a fistful of his dark hair and kissed him.

This was not right, kissing her former boyfriend less than an hour after her husband had died. After she'd killed him. It was completely wrong.

Liv pulled away. "I'm so sorry."

"Don't be sorry. You're upset. And scared."

"That's no excuse! This is wrong!" She stepped back a few feet. "I'm trying to figure out what to do. Should I call the police? Should I just leave?"

"Go to the elders," Isaac suggested.

"No. Not after what happened with my family. I just want to leave and get out of here. I'm afraid they won't believe it was self-defense. Jake was so nice to everyone. Who would believe that he was abusive?"

"You should have come to me and told me what was happening." He took a step towards her. "I could have helped you."

"That wouldn't have been right." She crossed her arms over her body.

"Maybe you should go see Diana."

"I did. You know what she told me? She said she didn't even believe me!"

His eyes widened. "I'm so sorry, Liv."

He was going to try to hug her again, and she didn't want her mind clouded any more than it was. She backed away, tears threatening.

"I'm leaving Unity forever. I'm not good at being Amish. I never will be. I don't belong here."

"You're leaving?" he whispered, his face paling.

"There is no way I could live here after this. If no one believes he was abusing me, they won't believe he tried to kill me, and they'll shun me for defending myself. I just want to go somewhere else and start over. So many terrible things have happened to me here. So many bad memories haunt me."

Isaac just stared at her, tears filling his eyes.

"Come with me, Isaac. Let's leave and never come back."

"I—I can't do that."

"Why not?"

"My family is here. And my work. This place is my life. I'd be lost without it." He raised his palms.

"Don't you want to be with me?" A tear crept down her cheek. "After all this time, we finally have a second chance. Jake is out of the picture. We could start over. Come with me! Out there, we can be together."

Maybe this was happening too fast.

He grabbed her hand. "We could be together here too."

"No. I can't stay here. My family was killed here, and being here reminds me of it every day. Do you love this place more than me?"

"Liv, it's not that simple!" he cried. "I could never leave this place. It's my home. I belong here."

"Fine. I hate this place. If you really want to stay here, that's okay. I guess we were never meant to be." She had to get out of there.

Besides, this was wrong.

Everything about this was wrong. Shame filled her, making her heart and feet heavy as she turned away.

"I have to go," she mumbled.

She stormed out, her heart breaking. She left Isaac standing there, staring at her as she stomped away.

Maybe what they shared was an infatuation after all, remnants from their time together as teens. It hadn't been real, just an illusion. They had just been caught up in the moment.

And he was right. He did belong there. This was for the best.

Liv blushed at the memory and brought herself back to the present. Shame and embarrassment washed over her. Had she really done that? Had she really kissed Isaac and asked him to leave with her that day? Maybe Jake's death had rattled her more than she thought. Later on, she realized she had been wrong and asked the Lord for forgiveness.

Since then, she had tried to forget about it and act like it had never happened. But this situation brought back the memories and pain all over again.

Now, as she drove, she pushed the memories out of her mind.

Liv looked in the rear view mirror, noting a black car with no license plates following them. Had it been there for a while and she hadn't noticed? These back roads seemed to go on and on, and one car could easily follow another for miles without meaning to.

Apprehension stirred within her. Why would someone be following them? Had the car been following them ever since they left the hospital and she had been too distracted to notice?

Perhaps they were trying to get to Isaac, or if they knew she was a detective on the case, maybe they wanted to stop her.

She made a sharp left, hoping that the car would keep on going straight, but they followed her.

"This is not the way to our houses," Isaac told her, confusion in his tone.

"I know. I think that car is following us. I'm seeing if they are."

She made a right, then several more turns. Though the car fell back a little, it still followed.

"They definitely are." She stomped on the gas, and they flew down the road, then the roar of the engine behind them grew louder and louder as it got closer and closer. She glanced in her rear view mirror again, and this time the car was close enough to hit them.

Wham!

Liv's car jolted forward and Isaac let out a yelp, clutching his neck and head in pain as the impact snapped his already sore head backward, then forward. The car behind them rammed into them again, probably bashing in Liv's back fender, but that was the least of her worries. After one final smash, the black car accelerated and drove beside them in the opposite lane. If another car came around the bend, there would be a head-on collision.

The driver, wearing a ski mask, rolled down his window and shouted in a gravelly voice, "Pull over!"

Liv thought of the weapon in her leg holster. Should she shoot at their attacker's tires and blow her cover? Or try to outrun him?

She couldn't blow her cover this early on. It would ruin the entire investigation. She had to outrun him.

The black car slammed against the side of her vehicle, disrupting her chaotic thoughts. Fury welled up inside her, especially at the thought of how he could easily kill someone any second as a result of his reckless driving.

"Hold on, Isaac!"

Liv slammed on the brakes, completely throwing the black car off. She whipped the car to the left and swerved onto a side road, then took several random turns in hopes of losing the other driver. When she was finally sure they had lost him, she slowed down the car's speed.

"What—What just happened?" Isaac massaged the back of his neck.

"I don't know." She let out the breath she hadn't realized she'd been holding, her pulse slowing to a normal rate again.

"We must leave it all in the Lord's hands and not worry."

"Yes. You're right. All that matters is we're both alive."

Yeah. For now. Did this person think that Isaac knew information that could incriminate him? Or did he not know that Isaac remembered nothing of the attack? And that even if Isaac did remember, that he wouldn't tell the police anything?

Liv wasn't sure, but either someone wanted to scare Isaac into remaining silent, or they were trying to scare Liv away.

Good thing she didn't scare easily.

Chapter Six

"Want me to go with you to your aunt's and uncle's house? Then you could take me home," Isaac suggested from the passenger seat of the car.

Liv considered her options. *It might make things less awkward if I have someone else with me.*

"Sure. Thanks." She didn't bother faking a smile as she turned her car onto the dirt road that led to the Mast farm. Fields still partly covered in snow stretched out before them, and one field fenced in several horses. Soon the snow would melt and the fields would come alive with green and the colors of wildflowers, and Aunt Mary would plant her garden.

Aunt Mary and Uncle Gideon had always been there for her, along with their sweet daughter Maria.

"We will always love you," her Uncle Gideon had told her, his chocolate brown eyes filling with tears. She had been so confused, trying to figure out what to do—leave Jake or try to work things out for the thousandth time.

"If you want to leave Jake, temporarily or permanently, you are always welcome here," Aunt Mary had offered.

That meant a lot, considering Liv could be shunned for leaving Jake and then Uncle Gideon, Aunt Mary, and Maria would be shunned for speaking to her. Olivia had felt so loved that she had sobbed in their arms. They had always loved her so much, and she had left them abruptly. She hadn't had the guts to tell them to their faces that she was leaving. A stab of guilt ripped her insides as she tried to imagine their reaction to the letter she had left, thanking them for all they had done for her and explaining why she had to leave.

Tears stung her eyes at her cowardice. They must have been so shocked and devastated.

She wanted to make it up to them, but she couldn't. In fact, she'd hurt them all over again when her assignment was over and she left. Again. She'd have to lie to them about wanting to rejoin the church. But it was the only way she would be able to get the information she needed to catch the criminal.

She bit her lip to keep from crying. Dread settled like a brick in her chest as she thought of the day she would have to leave again.

She pushed those thoughts out of her mind. That was all out of her control. For now, she had to apologize to her relatives and focus on keeping her cover and doing her job.

And not falling for Isaac again.

She sure had her work cut out for her.

Liv pulled into the drive. She had to face this just like any other mission she was assigned. *Just do it and get it over with.*

She helped Isaac out of the car and led him to the front door, feeling the warmth of his hand on her arm and the heat oozing through her body like warm honey. But it was the last thing on her mind. She stared at the front door.

Would they still welcome her? After all these years when she had made no effort to contact them? No phone calls, no letters… It had been too painful for Liv to talk to them after she had left, so she had slashed all ties to this place.

The door seemed to grow larger with every step they took toward it, and for a moment Olivia feared it would swallow her whole. She silently chided herself on her foolishness.

When they approached it, Liv hesitated, so Isaac knocked.

She wished she could have called before showing up like this, but like the other Amish families, the Masts didn't have a phone in their house. There were only phones in the phone shanties and in businesses, and she'd have to rely on someone taking them a message, revealing her arrival to others before she was ready. Besides, they probably wouldn't have gotten the message in time.

The door opened, and Maria stood there. She was no longer the child Liv remembered. Her cousin was now a beautiful, tall young woman with big brown eyes and brown hair peeking out from under her head covering. Instantly, her hands flew to her mouth and she shrieked, "*Mamm!* Come quick! Olivia's home!" Then she threw her arms around Olivia, who almost lost her balance. Liv held onto Maria tightly as memories of when she had lived in this house came rushing back, along with feelings of joy and safety.

Aunt Mary came running to the door in a frenzy, calling Olivia's name, waving a damp dish towel. She threw herself onto Olivia, tears running down her face. Isaac leaned against the railing and smiled.

"Oh, you're back!" Aunt Mary kept saying, crying into Olivia's shoulder. Olivia wrapped her arms around her aunt, knowing she was about to cry as well.

Yes, she was happy to see her relatives. But her tears of joy mingled with tears of guilt.

Before they stepped apart, she worried one of them would feel her gun beneath the layers of her dress as they embraced. So she pulled away, already missing the warmth and love of Aunt Mary's arms around her.

"Come in, come in! We have so much to talk about!" Aunt Mary ushered her inside. "You're just in time for dinner. Gideon will be home soon. He'll be so glad to see you." She seemed to notice Isaac for the first time. "Isaac, would you like to stay for dinner?"

"Yes, thank you. Then Liv will take me home so I can see my family."

"Excellent. Come in."

Aunt Mary's hair was almost entirely gray and white beneath her *kapp*. When Liv left, it had been a light brown with only a few streaks of gray.

So much could happen in six years.

They walked into the kitchen, which was exactly how it had been the day she had left. The wooden cabinets made by Uncle Gideon, the bright sunroom with large windows, the black wood stove radiating heat, and the simplicity of the almost bare walls brought back memories of when she had lived there. The window at the kitchen sink overlooked the fields and trees.

The wooden, handcrafted, rustic table still had four seats. How many times had they thought of her over the years while looking at the empty fourth chair?

Aunt Mary had a large pot of stew simmering on the wood stove, and the smell of bread baking in the oven wafted to Olivia the second she stepped inside. She had baked so many breads, apple dumplings, and pies with Aunt Mary and Maria in this kitchen. How she had missed such wonderful, homemade food. It was so much better than the frozen foods and takeout she had become accustomed to.

"Sit down. Tell me everything. What have you been doing all this time? What made you come back? Are you here to stay?" Aunt Mary poured out the questions like the tea she from her teapot. She slid a mug of lemon tea toward Olivia. Lemon was Liv's favorite, and Aunt Mary had remembered. Maria pulled her chair closer to Liv's and sat down, eagerly awaiting a reply.

"I've been working at a local restaurant in Portland, saving up money. I wasn't really sure what I was going to do from there, but I realized the *Englisher* life was not for me. It is so empty." She blew on her tea and hoped she was a good liar.

"Indeed. I'm just so glad you're back, dear. Oh, I'm so sorry to neglect you, Isaac. How are you feeling after your accident?" Aunt Mary gave him a mug.

It was an attack. There's a big difference. But the Amish would refer to his attack—any attack—as an incident or accident.

"I had a concussion, but I'm doing well now. Except I can't remember what happened that night. Liv thinks my memory might come back now that I am home and around familiar surroundings." Isaac warmed his thick fingers on the mug.

"I pray it does." Aunt Mary nodded.

"So the *Englisher* life is not all you thought it would be?" Maria asked as her eyes widened. She pulled her chair a little closer to Liv.

"No. People have cars, nice things, and fancy homes, and they are always communicating on phones and computers. But it's all so impersonal. Here, on these farms, even though it takes longer to visit someone and you can't text or email your friends, you're all so much closer to each other. There is a bond of community and friendship here so strong you can sense it. In the *Englisher* world, people usually only care about themselves. Here, you all take care of each other." A frown pulled down her smile. "Most of the time."

Silence overshadowed the room for a moment.

"I am so sorry about what happened, Liv." Aunt Mary walked over and rested a hand on Olivia's arm. "I understand why you had to leave."

"When Jake died, I couldn't face anyone. I'm sorry I didn't say goodbye." Usually confident, Liv couldn't look her aunt in the eye.

"It's all right. We got the letter."

"I was so afraid, and I left so quickly. I know people here try not to judge others, but how can one not judge a woman who killed her husband when they don't know the full story? I didn't think people would believe me, and I didn't blame them for it because no one knew the truth about Jake. I know I would never... I mean, I *knew* I wouldn't fit in. Besides, my family died here. I just didn't see any other option."

"We really do understand," Maria said in a soothing voice.

Liv stubbornly blinked back tears. "I went to court after I left. The jury ruled it self-defense when they saw the pictures of the bruises on my body and the marks on my neck, and when they heard Isaac and me testify."

Aunt Mary nodded. "Maybe you should explain what happened to the church."

Liv snorted out a laugh. "Diana and Samuel would love that."

"That's a tricky situation. People should know the truth, but you're right. They won't like people to know Jake was abusive toward you," Isaac said. "I think you should tell the truth, Liv, so people understand why you protected yourself. Besides, the Bible says to speak the truth."

"You're right. On Sunday, when I repent, I will tell the story."

The front door opened and Uncle Gideon stood in the doorway. His eyes met Liv's and he froze. He let out a sob and ran into the kitchen with his muddy boots still on.

This time, Liv couldn't maintain her tough composure. She held onto his shirt and bit her lip, trying to keep the tears away, but she couldn't stop them. She had only seen Uncle Gideon cry maybe once or twice in her life. He rarely cried, but when he did, Liv always cried, too.

He squeezed her in his arms so tight she thought she might break, but she didn't mind. A sense of home enveloped her, and she wished she could stay here forever.

She had forgotten what home felt like. What family felt like.

What love felt like. To be loved—it was such a powerful thing. And since she had left Unity, she had been starved of it. For the past six years she had had no family, no close friends, and no true home, only an empty apartment.

And her career. It had been everything to her. And it still was. She loved her job. It was why she got up every morning—to help people, to rescue people.

To arrest guys like the one who killed Bill Sullivan and knocked out Isaac. She wanted to arrest attackers like those so they couldn't hurt anyone else.

*

After an evening of reminiscing and catching up, Liv took Isaac home. The drive took less than a minute, but she didn't want him walking home in his condition.

"Still looks the same as when I left." Liv gestured to his small wooden house and pulled into the dirt driveway. Even though the Amish of Unity didn't have cars, they still used driveways for their buggies and for *Englisher* visitors who had cars.

"It was nice of all the men to pitch in to help me build this. It's small, but it's just me, so it's good enough."

Something in her heart fluttered. He wasn't married. Why hadn't a nice man like Isaac found a woman yet? How many admirers did he have? Surely all the young single women had their eyes on him. Was he interested in any of them in return?

"Thanks for staying. It was good to have you there." She tapped the steering wheel awkwardly.

"No problem. I'm glad I could help. It's really good to have you back. I missed you." He turned toward her.

Just get out of the car, Isaac. She needed space before this got out of hand and he tried to kiss her.

I can't believe he missed me.

The tender thought almost made her let her guard down, but she caught herself. She cleared her throat. "Well, thanks again. Good night," she said, finality in her tone.

"Good night."

"Need help?"

"No, I'll be okay."

Liv didn't ask him if he was sure, but she kept a close eye on him as he hobbled to his front door.

Liv backed out of the driveway and drove down the lane. She found herself driving to where her childhood home used to be before it had burned down. She got out of the car and stood at the edge of the road, staring into the openness.

Now it was just a field, but all those years ago it had been a thriving, colorful farm. Her father had been a farmer who took his produce to the local grocery store. Her mother had been an avid gardener and a hard worker. The house had always been alive with chatter and delightful chaos, the good kind of chaos, as it had sheltered her and her five siblings—Joe, Marcia, Heather, Allen, and blonde little Beth. Beth had only been five...

A sob choked Olivia as she stared at the empty land. The charred remains were no longer visible. The community had cleaned it up years ago. All that remained was the old foundation. Someone had planted some flowers. Someday, would someone else build a new house there?

Maybe, if things had turned out differently, she would have been living in a house there by now—with Isaac. Maybe with kids of their own.

Yes, that was what would have happened if she had not fallen for Jake. Her heart twisted with the thoughts of *what if?*

No. She couldn't ask herself that. Just like what she told victims and their families, *what ifs* will drive you crazy. It would be better to not think about it.

As she stared at where her house used to be, the memories of the night of the fire slowly leaked into her mind like kerosene. She had been coming home late one night after sneaking out again, and she had seen the smoke before she had seen the house. Flames devoured her home like a roaring lion.

The closest neighbors at the time were several fields away, too far away to notice in time, and sound asleep. And her father had been against smoke detectors, the very thing that could have saved the lives of his family.

She remembered running around the corner, past the trees and the barn, to see the house in flames. No neighbors lived near enough to hear her scream pierce the night. What should she do?

Should I go in and try to get them out or should I call the fire department?

She screamed again, this time in frustration. Valuable seconds ticked on while she deliberated. There was no way a petite sixteen-year-old girl like herself would be able to rescue them all.

Her vision tunneled, her heart rate increased. Nausea set in. A panic attack overwhelmed her. She tried to take deep breaths, tried to keep herself from passing out—she wouldn't be able to run if she was unconscious. Once she finally regained her composure enough, she turned to run to the phone shanty.

A figure moved slowly away from the house.

"*Daed*?" Was that him? Why was her father moving so slowly, so carefully, while his family was trapped inside a burning house? Or maybe it was a neighbor.

He froze, then turned toward her. This man was definitely not her father or a neighbor. She gasped when she saw the strange angry-clown mask on his face, and he held up something small and rectangular. Was that a box of matches? It was hard to tell from a distance. Confirming her suspicions, the man opened the box and lit one while staring at her. Chills crawled down her spine, and she felt as though all the blood was draining from her body.

Fear gripped her, and all she could do was stare back at him.

Who was that? Why was he doing this? Who was still alive? A dozen questions swarmed through her mind like angry ravens.

Then he darted away and escaped into the darkness.

She sprinted down the lane to the nearest phone shanty and dialed 911 with shaking fingers.

But she was too late. The trucks were too late.

No one survived…except her and the elusive arsonist.

Liv had wanted to let the police investigate, but the bishop would not allow her to answer their questions.

"This tragedy was God's will. It is up to Him to bring vengeance, not us. Leave it in God's hands, Olivia," Bishop Johnson had said, his beard bobbing. "We should not answer their questions about the fire."

She wanted to shake his shoulders as if to wake him up from a trance. "My entire family is *dead*! You expect me to just go on and live my life with no answers? I want to know who set my house on fire!"

"I understand, Olivia. But sometimes God does not give us the answers we want. Now, please, if you cannot contain yourself, I will ask you to leave. You must forgive the arsonist and move on. It is the Amish way. Do not hold bitterness in your heart."

Liv stood up from the table where they had been sitting, practically knocking her chair over. She hadn't been able to forgive the person who killed her family.

She never could.

A twig snapped in the woods somewhere in the distance, bringing Liv back to the present with a jolt. She whipped around and put her hand on her leg holster, listening intently as a breeze blew over her, sending chills shivering all over her body, rustling and shuffling the leaves on the trees like small green paper hearts. Another branch crunched, closer this time. She moved carefully to her car.

"I'm watching you, Olivia." The scratchy, deep masculine voice rode on the breeze from somewhere in the trees that no longer seemed so far from her. Her blood froze, a sick feeling churning in her gut. Was it the same voice as the man in the black car? The voice was so deep and gravelly that it sounded as if he was trying to make his voice sound different on purpose.

"You still mourn the ones who died here, don't you? You miss your family."

She stood on the other side of her vehicle, using it as protection as she carefully drew her M&P Shield. Her throat closed up. She wanted to shout angry words, accusations and questions, but fear stole her voice.

How did he know about the fire?

"You never did find the arsonist. That must eat at you."

Every day it did, but he didn't have to know that. She clicked the gun's safety off.

"Why did you come back here after all these years?" he asked.

She definitely couldn't answer that question. She clutched the pistol tighter, searching the darkness for any sign of movement, but it was as if no one was there. As if she was imagining things.

"If you go, I won't harm you. You should leave now while you still have the chance."

"No way," she muttered.

"What was that?" he asked, his tone condescending and sinister.

"I said there's no way I'm leaving!" she screamed, wanting to raise her weapon and fire a few warning shots, but she couldn't. She clenched her fists, her nails cutting into her palms.

"That's a nice fender you got there. You really should be more careful. You never know what sort of accidents could occur, especially if you're going to stay here."

This *was* the same man who had crashed into them on the road here!

So he had followed them here after all the precautions she had taken. The desire to arrest him burned hotter and fiercer within her.

Was this the same man who had killed Bill Sullivan?

Her heart pounded as she listened to him, incensed with his threatening words. She had to stay. If she left, there would be no investigation, no way for this man to be caught.

"Leave right now. Get in your little beat up car and drive home."

"It's going to take a lot more than a few threats to scare me." She stood up straighter and allowed her voice to carry over the field.

"You'll see that I'm not bluffing, dear."

That was it. She couldn't stand there any longer and listen to this narcissist. She tore off toward the voice in the woods, sprinting as hard as she could, pumping her legs until she reached the woods. When she entered into the canopy of the trees, she stopped and listened, shining the light on her cell phone.

But no one was there. He was already gone.

She spent a few more minutes searching but quickly gave up. Then she got back in her car and slammed the door in frustration. When she pulled into the Masts' driveway, she went inside quietly, since everyone was in bed. She plugged her cell phone into an outlet Uncle Gideon had in the basement for charging the rechargeable batteries for his battery-operated things. It was the only source of electricity in the entire house, and she was grateful her relatives had it in their home.

Upstairs, she undressed and yanked her *kapp* off. She removed her holster and put it and the gun in the drawer of the bedside table. Then she put on her pajamas, sat in the chair by the window, and stared into the night.

Liv could see where her old house used to be in the distance, and next door was the Sullivan house. From here she could see almost their entire yard.

She scanned the Masts' yard for any sign of movement, but she saw nothing.

Who was this man? He was probably middle aged or younger and pretty athletic, since he got away so quickly. And Liv could run pretty fast.

How did he know about the fire? Since the Amish were opposed to investigating crimes against them, the fire was never reported.

Was the killer an Amish man? How else would he know so much about her family's death? Perhaps the news had spread throughout the town to the outsiders.

How could she forget and call it an "incident" like the rest of the community when she knew it had been an unpunished murder? They had all been able to forgive, but she held on to the bitterness in her heart.

Rage burned within her as the mysterious man's words plagued her mind, filling her brain with the black smoke of anger. So many questions rose up from the darkness. She had to catch him. She wouldn't be at peace until she did.

Liv sat there for several minutes, then gave up and fell on the bed. She tucked herself in and rested the pistol on the blanket beside her, something she always did. It made her feel safe just knowing it was there.

If she caught anyone sneaking around or trying to hurt another victim, they'd be sorry.

Chapter Seven

Early the next morning, Olivia heard the sounds of Aunt Mary cooking breakfast, her humming, pots and pans clanging harmoniously, and bacon sizzling on the stove. Liv had forgotten how big a production breakfasts were here. It was normal for a family to have eggs, bacon, sausage, and homemade biscuits or pancakes on a daily basis. She'd grown accustomed to eating a granola bar or a banana on her way to work, if anything.

She rolled over and looked at the battery-operated clock. Seven o'clock. Aunt Mary had probably been up for a while. Liv pulled her blankets up around her, and her eyes slowly began to close again as the memories of the night before began slowly coming back.

"Come on, Olivia, time for breakfast!" Maria stuck her head in the doorway.

The gun!

Olivia panicked and quickly threw her covers over the weapon on the mattress beside her, but Maria was gone in a flash of pink skirts and clearly hadn't noticed it. Liv had not expected a family member to come barging into her room. She should have, because Maria had done it often when they were growing up, but Olivia was used to living alone now.

Sighing in relief, she knew she would have to be more careful, but she needed it near her as she slept. She got up and dressed, adjusting her holster, then hurried to the basement to retrieve her phone, making sure it was on silent and also hiding it in her holster. She couldn't very well pretend to want to be Amish again with her phone going off in church.

Church. Great. She sighed, not looking forward to what would most likely be a three-hour sermon in both English and Pennsylvania Dutch. She remembered most of the latter language because, like most Amish children, she had learned it before she had learned English.

The family shared a lively breakfast and sang a hymn after eating. Then Uncle Gideon read a passage from the Bible. Liv tried to act like she was paying attention, but she almost nodded off at the table.

They piled into the buggy and set off on the fifteen-minute ride to church. It was a beautiful day, about fifty degrees, and the snow was melting.

Maria looked lovely in her light pink dress, but Liv didn't say so. She knew compliments on beauty made Amish women uncomfortable. But no doubt about it, Maria was beautiful. Anyone could see that. Her brown hair was pinned back perfectly, and her chestnut eyes were framed by long, dark eyelashes above perfect cheekbones.

"So is there anyone special in your life, Maria?" Liv asked.

"Oh, yes! I am dating Robert Lapp." She grinned.

"He is such a nice young man," Aunt Mary added.

"I love him very much." Maria sighed. "We plan on getting married one day."

"I'm really happy for you." Liv sincerely meant it.

They pulled into the churchyard, which was already almost full, and Liv's heart rate doubled. How would people respond to her?

Maria must have sensed Liv's anxiety, and she squeezed her hand. "It will be okay. I think they will understand. Even if they don't believe it was self-defense, they should be forgiving."

Olivia forced a smile at Maria's attempt at comforting her. She shouldn't care what these people thought about her. She wasn't staying long anyway.

They walked into the church, which was a two-story building. The bottom floor was where everyone ate, and the second floor was divided into two parts—the church and the school. They walked upstairs, and Liv hoped no one would recognize her. But her appearance had hardly changed in the last several years, except her hair, which was covered.

As the Mast family made their way into the church area, a few people stopped their conversations and stared at her. Then they looked away, trying not to be rude.

Except Diana and Samuel Sullivan, who narrowed their eyes at her. Olivia boldly stared right back at them, and their cold glares rekindled the anger she had felt when Diana had blamed Liv for Jake's abuse. They were the only Amish people she knew who would ever behave in such a way. They were the only bitter people in the community. Every other Amish person Liv knew was kindhearted and merciful. But the Sullivans were the exception to the rule. They had always been an unhappy family.

"What is *she* doing here?" Diana whispered.

The Amish were all about forgiveness, but maybe murder was unforgivable. And from the looks that a few people were now giving her, she knew instantly that Diana and Samuel, Jake's brother, had tried to make everyone believe that Liv had murdered Jake in cold blood.

Because they didn't want to admit that Jake had been abusive. Good Amish men were never cruel or abusive. But Jake had not been a good Amish man, had he?

"Everyone, please take your seats!" Bishop Johnson called. Seeing him brought back memories of him encouraging her to forgive the arsonist who had killed her parents and siblings. Though she had tried, she had never been able to.

He began with an opening prayer, then asked if there were any announcements. Captain Branson's orders rang through her head, how he had asked her to ask the community to accept her again. She knew this was her chance, so she stood up.

"Bishop Johnson, if I may, I would like to ask the church for forgiveness," she said.

He looked shocked for a moment when he recognized her, then he motioned for her to come forward. "By all means. Certainly."

As she stood up and made her way to the front, she felt people staring at her. The silence wrapped around her like a damp blanket. But she ignored the awkwardness as she stood in front of the congregation of eighty or so people.

"Good morning." She clasped her hands together, feigning meekness, keeping her eyes low. What she really wanted to do was tell them all about the importance of justice, and how the fire and Jake's crimes should have been investigated. They thought they were doing what was best, but she knew so much more about the law now.

"As many of you may know, I am Olivia Mast. I mean—" She had changed her last name back to Mast after she had left. "I was Olivia Sullivan, but it's Olivia Mast now. I left on bad terms, and I want to apologize for how I handled things back then. I would like to explain why I killed my late husband, Jake Sullivan."

Murmurs resounded through the room, and without waiting for permission, she continued boldly.

"I'm sorry to tell you that Jake abused me throughout our entire marriage, as some of you may now know. I killed him in self-defense. I went to court after, and I was found not guilty. I can prove it. There was plenty of evidence of his abuse, including several injuries he gave me, especially when he tried to strangle me. I am sorry I killed him, and I ask you all for your forgiveness. I would like to become Amish again, if you all will accept me. Like the prodigal son."

She added that last bit for dramatic effect. And maybe if she related her experience to a Bible story, they would feel more sympathetic toward her. Sure, it would be nice to have everyone's forgiveness, but she hated lying. Especially to her aunt, uncle, and Maria.

"But she killed my son!"

Olivia turned to see Diana, face red with anger where she sat. Of course Diana had to go and ruin this.

Samuel added, "Who knows what else she is capable of?"

What? Was he implying that she could have killed Bill Sullivan?

She was here to catch the killer, not to become the suspect!

"I told you," she said in a calm voice. "It was self-defense. He was choking me. Ask the police or the judge. They can prove it. They have records and evidence. If I hadn't done what I did, I'd be dead. Just ask them."

Some had shocked looks on their faces. Samuel and Diana scowled at her. They couldn't deny the truth when there was proof.

And they knew the truth.

"So will you accept me back?" she asked the group as nicely as she could.

She waited. Some of the people before her looked down when she made eye contact. Some of them whispered among themselves. Some looked at her in consideration.

Uncle Gideon stood up. "Don't you all think she should have a second chance? She's been through so much, and she needs our community. We are all sinners and God forgave us. God says if we do not forgive others, He will not forgive us."

Leave it to Uncle Gideon. She was thankful for him speaking up, even if she did not really think she had sinned by killing Jake in self-defense.

"I agree," Isaac said, standing up. Maria stood up, then Isaac's entire family stood in agreement. Slowly and gradually, the entire congregation was standing, *kapps* or beards bobbing as people nodded, except for Diana and Samuel, who turned red where they sat.

"Well, Olivia Mast, welcome back into the community," Bishop Johnson said.

"Thank you." Guilt overflowed out of her in the form of a few tears that crept down her cheek, which the congregation probably assumed were tears of joy and gratefulness. Her stomach clenched, and she tried not to let her face reveal her true emotions as she made her way back to her seat.

After the sermon, Liv went downstairs with everyone else for lunch. Women began setting out homemade food over several long tables, including pies, sandwiches, salads, and casseroles. Now most of them smiled at her warmly, saying hello and telling her they were glad she was home.

As the women scurried around busily preparing the food, Liv was about to walk around a corner when she heard her name, so she stopped.

"Why do you think Olivia came back after all these years in the *Englisher* world?"

"Probably because she couldn't show her face for so long after killing my son." That was Diana's cold voice.

"She made everyone think my son abused her and tried to kill her. But she killed him wrongly."

"Really? So she made up rumors about Jake?" asked a third voice.

"Yes. I don't like having her around here. I don't trust her."

"Well, if she didn't kill Jake because he was abusive, why did she kill him then? What about the judge and the evidence?"

"She must have twisted the truth to make them think she was innocent. She probably killed him so she could be with Isaac Troyer. They dated not long before she married Jake. Maybe Olivia regretted

Jake and wanted him out of the picture so she could marry Isaac."

It took everything in Liv to not stomp over to them and set them straight. She fumed silently, clenching her fists. She couldn't remember ever hearing an Amish person gossip before. Normally, people in the community did not engage in such behavior, but no one was perfect.

"Well, then, why didn't they get together after?" one voice asked.

"He probably couldn't stand the thought of being with her after he found out she viciously murdered her husband. He was probably afraid of her."

How dare they talk about her like that? And why did they have to bring Isaac into it?

So was that what Diana was letting everyone believe? That Olivia killed Jake so she could be with Isaac?

Her face heated in anger, and she wanted to rip off her *kapp* and leave town. Instead, she decided she would question Diana right then and there.

Liv stepped out from where she had been listening and watched the women's faces as they realized she had heard everything. Liv smiled at them in a sugary-sweet way.

"Good morning, ladies. You have all made me feel so welcome here," she said, trying not to sound sarcastic. She watched them all blush and squirm, looking like they wanted to crawl under their seats like frightened insects. Served them right for saying such things about her. And in church, for Pete's sake!

"Oh, well, I have to go," one of them mumbled, then they all scrambled away like skittish mice.

Diana started to leave, but Liv grabbed her arm. "Wait. I have some questions for you."

"What?" Diana muttered, still looking a little embarrassed.

"Well, first of all, I wanted to express my condolences and say I'm sorry for your loss." She paused. "I was also wondering if you saw or heard anything peculiar the night Bill was murdered."

"No." Obviously annoyed, Diana crossed her arms in front of her. "A lot of trees were falling that night because of the wind, and it was loud, so I didn't even hear the gunshot." Diana's voice was void of sorrow even though her husband had just died. Liv had always suspected Bill Sullivan was abusive just like Jake, so maybe Diana was relieved she was now single.

"Did anyone unusual come around that day? Was anything odd to you?" Liv prodded.

"No! Why are you asking me such things?" Diana snapped. Liv had been wondering where her cold demeanor had gone.

"Just curious." Liv shrugged. "It's odd to me that no one saw anything or even heard anything."

"It's none of your concern. Now leave me alone, please." Diana shoved past her.

Well, it *was* Liv's concern. And she'd do what she had to do to get some answers.

"Oh, hi, Olivia! Remember me, Annaliese Hersberger?" Anna grinned at her.

Liv really wanted to just ignore her and walk away. Anna was a sweet woman, but Liv didn't feel like talking to anyone. She forced herself to be polite anyway. "Oh, yes, I do. How are you, Anna?"

"Great," Anna said with a grin, her blue eyes twinkling. Her blonde hair was perfectly twisted back under her *kapp*. She was beautiful and sweet and probably a near perfect Amish woman.

"Well, then, if there is nothing else..." Liv started to move away.

"I just wanted to thank you for bringing Isaac home. We are basically dating, and I was so worried about him. I was going to arrange with his parents to get a driver for him, but you saved us the trouble. Thank you again."

Dating? Liv's heart plummeted. Isaac was dating this Amish Barbie? Of course he was. What man wouldn't want to date her?

Could this day seriously get any worse?

Something inside Olivia fell apart, and tiny shards of demolished hope stabbed her insides.

"You're welcome. Excuse me." Liv walked away and sat near Aunt Mary, away from everyone else so she could be alone.

She propped her elbows on the table and rested her chin in her hands. Why did she feel so devastated? There was no hope for her and Isaac. She'd be leaving soon, and she was sure Isaac would not come with her. He hadn't wanted to before, so why would he now?

She just wanted to get out of here, away from all these people. Her most important rule was to never let her job get personal, but maybe this was all too much. Swatting away a hot tear, she became annoyed with herself for getting so emotional. This was the hardest assignment she had ever had, and she had had some difficult, ugly, gruesome ones.

Branson wouldn't let her leave Unity without losing her job. She pictured the white sandy beaches again with the swaying palm trees and tried to relax.

When this was over and she caught the perp, she would leave. Once and for all. And she'd try to never think of this place again.

"Are you okay, Liv?" Aunt Mary asked, concern lining her voice.

Liv knew her aunt meant well, but she really wished people would just leave her alone. "I'm fine. This is all just a little overwhelming. In a good way." She gave a small smile.

"Well, here's some casserole." Aunt Mary handed her a plate. Despite her jealousy, disappointment and anger, she was hungry. And the food was delicious.

*

Isaac's thoughts ran wild. The church had accepted Liv into the community.

That meant that he could rightfully ask her uncle permission to court her. He looked over at her talking with the other women and couldn't help but smile. She was not the friendliest person, nor the sweetest, but something about her drew him as she chomped on her food and looked around with shifty eyes. She clearly still didn't trust anyone.

She was strong, and she was brave. And she did open her heart to some people, but it was rare. She had built so many walls to protect herself over the years, and he didn't blame her, but he had no idea how he would get past them. Her walls might keep out pain, but they could keep out love, too.

And he still loved her. He always had. How could he get her to trust him?

Diana's response to Olivia's request for forgiveness had been beyond harsh. His stomach clenched at the memory of seeing Liv's face after her former mother-in-law and brother-in-law had lashed out at her in front of everyone that morning. He had wanted to say something in Liv's defense, but he had no idea what to say. Thank God Gideon had stepped in.

He glanced at Liv again. She still wasn't talking to anyone. What was she upset about now? She had just been accepted back into the church. Wasn't that what she had wanted? Why wasn't she rejoicing?

Was she rethinking her decision?

"So... Olivia is back," Robert Lapp said, taking a step closer to Isaac.

"Yes."

"Do you still love her?" Robert asked quietly.

"Yes, I do." Isaac sighed.

"So you are going to ask her to date you?"

"I want to, but I'm not sure when."

"You and I have been friends for a long time, and after she left you talked so much about how you missed her. So maybe, if you still love her, you should. But what about Anna?"

"Anna's not my girlfriend. She's nice, but I never loved her like I love Liv." He had been talking with Anna lately. He was pretty sure she liked him, and he sensed that their families expected them to marry eventually. But he hadn't been able to bring himself to ask her out. He had always felt it wasn't right. As if he was waiting for something.

Or someone.

"Well, you better make it clear to Anna what your intentions are, because I think she thinks you two are dating," Robert said. "She probably thought you were just too shy to officially ask her to be your girlfriend."

The guilt for unintentionally leading Anna on weighed Isaac down. They had only talked, but she had taken it wrong. He'd have to talk to her soon and end whatever it was she thought was between them. He glanced over at her, and she smiled back sweetly. He hoped he wouldn't hurt her feelings too badly, but it had to be done.

And when the time was right, he intended to ask Liv to be his girlfriend.

*

About an hour later, people began to leave the church to go home or visit friends or relatives, as the Amish usually did on Sundays. Liv wandered outside, spotted Samuel, and figured she might as well talk to him sooner than later.

He was laughing with a few friends, but once they saw her they politely backed away.

"Good morning, Samuel."

"What do you want?" He crossed his arms like his mother had earlier.

"Look, I'm really sorry about your father. But I was just wondering if you had seen or heard anything odd or suspicious the night he was killed."

"No. Nothing at all. No one even heard the shot because of the wind knocking down trees. And we've already put it behind us. It doesn't help when you dig it up like this."

"Sorry. Do you know anything about what happened? It is just odd to me that no one witnessed anything. "

"Well, that's the way it happened. No one saw anything, and I don't know anything. Why are you asking so many questions? Please leave my mother and me alone. We are grieving—again—and we don't need you around to remind us of Jake and my father. Not to mention my brothers and sister who are no longer with us."

She wanted to grab him by the suspenders and scream that Jake's death wasn't her fault. She had only been protecting herself, and now she was just doing her job.

Then Liv remembered how much the callous man before her had lost. He'd lost his siblings and father—almost his entire family. All he had left was his mother. Liv bit back her protests and her heart softened a bit.

He glared at her again, huffed, and stomped away.

Okay, so no one had witnessed anything, unless they were lying. That was a big help.

Isaac and Uncle Gideon looked deep in conversation as Liv approached. Uncle Gideon patted Isaac on the back, and Isaac grinned like a fool. What on earth were they talking about?

Isaac turned to Liv. "Will you walk back with me, Liv?"

"Sure." Aunt Mary and Uncle Gideon left with Maria, and Isaac led Liv through a shortcut, a path through the woods that would lead to their houses. Since they weren't dating yet, their time alone would not be frowned upon.

It was a beautiful, warm day, a welcome change from the snowy days they had been having all winter in Maine. Sunlight shone through the trees and melted the remaining snow on the ground.

"Look, there are some robins over there. You know that means warmer weather is coming very soon." Isaac pointed to the orange-bellied birds chirping in the trees and hopping on the ground. "Finally."

"Oh, good. It seems like winter is seventy-five percent of the year in Maine," Liv said dryly.

"Definitely." He cleared his throat. "So… I'll just get to the point. Okay?"

"Go for it."

Isaac's heart pounded so hard it ached, and adrenaline coursed through him.

"I still love you. The truth is, I have always loved you, Liv."

There. He said it. He glanced at her to try and read her face. Liv kept on walking, staring ahead. Her eyes widened as she took a few deep breaths, looked at him and opened her mouth to say something, then stopped. She looked confused and torn, but he couldn't help but notice a little smile tugging on the corner of her lip. She was so beautiful.

This was the first time he had ever seen Olivia speechless.

"This probably is the completely wrong time to tell you this, with you moving back here and rejoining the church and all. I'm sorry if I overwhelmed you." He grimaced. His timing was terrible.

"Oh, it's okay. I'm glad you told me. It's good to be upfront and honest with people instead of hiding things." Was it just him, or was she clenching her jaw?

"I agree. I probably should have waited, though. I just could hardly wait to tell you. And I also would like to ask you, when you are ready, to be my girlfriend. I just asked Gideon's permission, and he gave it to me. But I understand if you need more time." His words tumbled out in a rush. He needed to speak his mind before he chickened out. So far, she took this all so well, and that relieved him.

"What about Anna?" she blurted. "Aren't you two dating? She told me you were." Liv's cheeks turned red. Was that a little bit of jealousy in her eyes?

"No. No, no. We are not dating. She might think so, but we aren't. I'm going to make myself clear to her soon. I started talking with her a little while ago, but it was because I was lonely. I didn't know where you were or if you were ever coming back. But I always knew I'd never love anyone as much as I love you. She's nice, but I didn't ever love her. I love *you*."

Liv took a deep breath. "Today has been full of surprises. Well, you better tell her that ASAP, because she seemed pretty enamored with you. I don't blame her." She gave him a rare smile.

His insides warmed with happiness. "So forget about her. This is about you and me. I'm guessing you're not ready to date me yet—"

"No. Not yet." Her voice was uncertain.

"How about if you let me know when you are? If that ever

happens."

    "Okay."

Chapter Eight

On the outside, Liv looked composed, but her pulse pounded in her ears. She couldn't believe she had just stupidly told him she would let him know when she was ready to date him.

Because, undeniably, that was what she truly wanted, more than a vacation in the Bahamas.

But it was impossible. It was as impossible as her catching every single criminal in Maine all by herself.

She knew he could sense that she had feelings for him. He knew her so well, she wouldn't be able to hide that from him.

She would have to talk to Branson about this. It would be good for her cover if she dated someone within the community, to establish trust, but then both of their hearts would be broken when she left.

Unless she could convince him to leave with her.

That was irrational. He would never leave. He obviously loved it here. It was his entire world. He'd never feel at home in her world, which was so full of violence and death and deceit.

They continued walking, and Liv realized they were near a cluster of Amish houses.

"Hey. Can you show me where Sid found you?" It was about time she quit letting herself get distracted and searched for clues instead.

"Sure. He showed me the spot."

They walked further down the lane past his house, and Isaac

stopped on the side of the road. "Sid found me here very early in the morning after I was assaulted. I don't even remember him taking me to the hospital."

Olivia looked around for anything that might help her in the case, like something the perp might have dropped or even a footprint. Something. Anything.

"Did anyone hear the gunshot when Bill was killed?" she asked.

"Actually, no one really did. It was very windy that night, and some trees fell, so it seems everyone thought the noise was from a tree falling, not a gun."

Great. Did the shooter have a silencer?

"I wonder if you fought back when you were hit."

"No. I wouldn't have done that. The Bible says—"

"To turn the other cheek. I know." Scanning the ground, she withheld a remark about how she would have knocked the guy out. After a few moments of silence, she looked up to see him staring at her in confusion. Oh. She was supposed to be acting Amish.

"You would have fought back, wouldn't you? Violence is not the Amish way," he explained in a soft voice.

Well, she wasn't Amish, so that rule didn't apply to her. If someone had attacked her like that, she would have fought back with everything she had.

"Sorry," she said sheepishly.

He shrugged, smiling a little. So he found her amusing?

On the ground was no sign of a struggle, but she did see marks in the dirt that looked like someone had been dragged. Had someone hit

Isaac then dragged him here?

The drag marks came from the direction of the Sullivans' house. She narrowed her eyes, wondering if someone would even bother covering up evidence when they thought no one would report their crimes. She'd have to sneak into the Sullivan house tonight to investigate. Hopefully, they were heavy sleepers.

"What are you thinking about?"

She smiled at him. "Nothing."

"I'm not convinced. Isn't that 'I don't want to talk about it' in female language?" Isaac laughed.

Let him think whatever he wants. "Yeah."

"Can I ask you a question?"

Something in her closed up. Her smile fell. No, she didn't want to talk about personal stuff like her past. But she found herself saying, "Sure."

"What happened the day you left? I mean, I know he tried to kill you so you killed him, but what is the full story?" Isaac stepped closer. He began walking further down the lane, away from the houses and toward the main road, and she walked beside him.

"I think you know Jake abused me for our entire marriage. It began as only verbal abuse, then escalated to include physical assault."

"You changed so much when you married him. You had been so full of life, then you were so withdrawn." He looked guilty, as if he had been the one who had hurt her, but it was because he hadn't been able to stop Jake.

She nodded slowly in agreement. "He watched us in the store, that day I ran into you and spilled my groceries. He saw us talking and the way…"

His eyes pleaded with her to go on.

She sighed and continued. "He saw how we were still friends, and he accused me of having an affair with you. I told him it wasn't true, but he must have convinced himself it was. So he hit me, then he tried to choke me. I had been chopping vegetables in the kitchen, and when I thought I was about to die, I grabbed the knife from behind me on the counter and stabbed him in the neck. After the fact, I realized I could have stabbed him somewhere where it wouldn't have killed him. But, in the moment, I was so angry and scared, and I just wanted him to stop. And it was one of the few places I could reach. It happened so fast. Maybe I wasn't thinking clearly." Her voice was flat, but inside she shuddered at the memories even though she had never regretted her decision to protect herself that day.

Then she'd gone to see Isaac right after Jake died. Her heart still ached when she remembered the way she had felt when he had refused to leave with her—so let down, so alone.

He reached for her hand, startling her out of her memories, and he didn't let go. She couldn't let go either. "I'm sorry, Liv" was his quiet answer.

"Don't be sorry. Bad things happen, and there are so many horrible people in this world. What matters is I survived, and I'm here today."

Isaac nodded. "I mean, I'm sorry I didn't go with you."

She stopped and looked at him, eyes wide and eyebrows raised. Did he really just say that?

"I was so scared of leaving this place. I just couldn't go with you. After you left, I regretted my decision every day. I wanted to go look for you, but I knew it was no use. I had no idea where you were, if you moved to another state... I just wonder what would have happened if—"

She put her hand up. "Don't ask yourself that. It really will make you nuts."

"Well, yes, it did. I just prayed every day for your return, and now you're here."

"You know, I might have had a big grudge against this community, but I never had anything against my family or you." She shifted her feet awkwardly.

"Liv, I never, ever want to lose you again. Never." His eyes intently stared into her own, and for the first time she realized he had a thin line of darkness around the edge of his irises. His usually green eyes looked almost brown in this light. His hair ruffled a little in the breeze, and she made herself look away.

"Anyway," she said a little too loudly, even though she hated to ruin the moment. Things were going a little too far. She was afraid he'd kiss her any second. "I bet Aunt Mary is wondering where we are. Let's go meet her at the house."

Since they had taken a shortcut from church, they arrived at about the same time as the buggy did. Robert, Maria, Aunt Mary, and Uncle Gideon piled out, and Gideon took the horse to the pasture.

"Will you stay and play games with us, Isaac?" Maria called, approaching them at the bottom of the stairs. "We'll play your favorite,

Dutch Blitz."

"I'd love to, Maria. Thank you. I could never pass up a game of Dutch Blitz. It's not often I get to play games with my pal Robert anymore, and I'd love to spend the afternoon with your wonderful family." He shot a heart-stopping smile at Liv, and she tried to stop the fluttering in her belly. She couldn't help but smile back, the corners of her mouth rising up rebelliously as if they had a mind of their own. Isaac started up the steps that led to the porch, and she followed behind with the others.

Isaac continued, "I have to warn you, though, it's been a while since I've played Dutch Blitz—"

His words were cut off as Isaac's foot fell through one of the steps, and though he reacted quickly and did not fall through, he fell forward on his hand and elbow, bumping his head on another step. He cried out in pain and surprise, then Liv was instantly at his side. The broken step had fallen to the ground, and Liv felt sick at the thought of Isaac almost falling that far.

"Are you all right?" She helped him up.

"What on earth happened?" Gideon's voice boomed from below as he hurried from the field and up the stairs, his gray beard bobbing with every step. "I made those steps myself, and they are much sturdier than that! And they were fine this morning when we walked on them."

Liv inspected the step more closely. It looked as though someone had sawed away at the wood and used glue to barely keep it together. Isaac's weight had broken it the rest of the way. Adrenaline washed through her veins, which was quickly poisoned by rage. Had the man from the woods who had threatened her and her relatives done this? The one who had threatened her when she refused to leave, telling her "accidents" could happen?

"I think I know what happened, and it has nothing to do with your excellent carpentry skills, Uncle Gideon," Liv stated, going up the rest of the way before them, testing out every board. The man who had threatened her must have done this while they were at church. She would grab the broken step later to have Jefferson pick it up and run it for prints.

"It doesn't matter who you think did it. The Lord calls us to forgive and forget. Let's not dwell on this," Gideon replied with a solemn voice.

But Liv couldn't forgive and forget. Isaac could have fallen and been seriously injured, or worse. The voice in the woods had not been bluffing after all.

When they reached the top of the stairs, everyone else went inside in search of the first aid kit and an ice pack. Liv tugged on Isaac's sleeve as he headed for the door, and he stopped and faced her. A bump and bruise were already forming above his left eye. She instinctively reached up her hand to touch his face, and he captured her hand with his own.

"Are you okay?" she asked. "You should go to the doctor."

"No, no, I'm all right. I caught my balance pretty quickly. Thank the Lord."

"Someone did this to you," she murmured, anger and determination to catch this killer heating her blood. "Anyone in my family could have been hurt."

"It doesn't matter. I'm all right, really. It's just a minor injury," he said in a smooth, deep voice. "Why do you think you have to figure all of this out? Why can't you just let the Lord handle it?"

"Sometimes I feel like I have to handle things myself." She was too afraid to trust anyone else. Even God. "You could have been killed. That step was high." Her voice cracked with emotion at the thought. Unshed tears of frustration burned her eyes, but she blinked them away.

"But I wasn't. The Lord protected me. Everything is all right. I don't want you to worry." Now he was the one touching her face, running a thumb along her jawline, then twirling one of the long, white ribbons on her *kapp*. "Promise me you will pray and cast your cares upon the Lord."

She only nodded, not sure if she could truly keep that promise. She wasn't ready to. Not yet.

"Well, are you two love birds going to play Dutch Blitz with us or what? We found the first aid kit!" Robert bellowed from the kitchen, and a few laughs followed his playful words.

"We better go in. Trust the Lord." Isaac's tone was gentle as he squeezed her hand reassuringly. She pondered his words.

Could she really trust God with the lives of her aunt, uncle, and cousin when they were the prey of a treacherous killer? Could He help her find and arrest this man, or did she really think she had to do it all on her own?

*

That evening, after a fun afternoon of games with Maria, Robert, Isaac, Aunt Mary, and Uncle Gideon, Olivia dropped off her car at a local diner where the owner said she could leave it for a few weeks, if she paid him something, so she did. She got a taxi back to the Mast house and went upstairs to her room, telling everyone she had sold her car. She finished unpacking the few bags she had brought with her.

The sun had not set yet. She looked out the window at the Sullivans' house.

There was something written on their basement window. From here, she couldn't read it, so she dug through her gear bag, pulled out her binoculars, and looked again.

She grabbed onto the windowsill and pressed her binoculars up against the glass, gasping.

Help was written on the window. With what, she couldn't tell, but one thing was for sure. There was something going on at the Sullivans' house. And she was going to find out what.

She wanted to run over there right then and kick down the door, but then she'd blow her cover and never find the killer. Or whoever was in that basement. No, she'd have to wait until the middle of the night to go inside quietly and look around without anyone finding out. The Amish here never locked their doors, so getting in wouldn't be a problem.

She had some time to kill, so she decided to give Branson an update. She walked out into the woods, took her phone out of her leg holster and placed the call.

"Liv, how goes it in Amishville?" he asked.

"It's interesting." She crushed some branches with her foot.

"Give me some info."

"Well, let's see." She told him about the car chase, the voice in the woods, and the stairs incident. "I didn't recognize the voice of the man when he threatened me, but it did sound like he was trying to disguise his voice, so it still could be someone I know.

"Also, I was accepted back into the community by the congregation at the church. No one seems to have heard the gunshot when Bill Sullivan was shot, so I don't have a witness as far as I know of yet.

"I looked at the site where Isaac Troyer was left after he was knocked unconscious, and it looks as though he was dragged to that spot from the Sullivan house. And, just now, I saw the word 'help' written on their basement window. I want to go investigate tonight. The Amish never lock their doors, so I figure I'll look around when everyone is asleep.

"Also, because Samuel was in church with us, he probably couldn't have tampered with the stairs while we were in church. Someone else had to have done it, so there could be two perpetrators. But I do think Samuel is up to something. There is definitely something going on at his house."

Branson said, "Okay. So, no witnesses, and someone might be locked in a basement. Since someone could be in immediate danger, you don't need a warrant because it is exigent circumstances. But do you think you need backup after all?"

"No. The killer will become suspicious if more people decide to randomly want to join the church because it's extremely rare. He would probably notice that and figure out that undercover detectives had been sent in, then he might lash out. And if you send officers, the community wouldn't like it. We would get nowhere. Just let me handle this, Captain."

"Fine, but you better call if something goes down. Anything else I should know?"

"Well, this is kind of personal, but I need some advice. Isaac Troyer just asked me to be his girlfriend. And dating here really means courting, which is dating with the intention of marriage. It's pretty serious. What should I do—you know—to keep my cover?" She felt guilty for talking to Branson about Isaac. Maybe it wasn't such a good idea.

"Date him. I mean, court him. That's great for your cover. It'll establish trust within the community."

That was not the answer she had really wanted to hear.

"In church, someone insinuated I could have killed Bill Sullivan— my mother-in-law and brother-in-law, who both hate me." She wrinkled her nose at the thought of them. "Even worse, they are telling people I killed my husband so I could be with Isaac Troyer."

"Not good. We don't want people suspecting you now that you have coincidentally shown up right after the murder. If you date this guy, he will trust you, so other people he knows will trust you. It's a good idea. Besides, you are supposed to be watching him because he could be on the killer's bad side. He might be our only witness, even if he doesn't remember it. Stay close to him, since he might be in the most danger. He lost his memory, but the killer might not know that, so he might want to scare him, hurt him, maybe even kill him."

"I won't let that happen." If something happened to Isaac she wouldn't be able to live with herself.

She wanted to groan. She rubbed her temples with her fingers and let out a deep breath. This was getting worse and worse. She was going to have to play Isaac like a pawn.

But then she'd leave, and he could marry Anna and forget about Liv and everyone would live happily ever after.

Maybe in a perfect world.

"Great. Okay. Anything else?" she asked.

"Jefferson keeps asking about you." She could tell by the sound of his voice he was smiling in amusement. "He's got it bad. He really likes you. Won't shut up about you."

"Tell him I'm fine." She really didn't want to talk about Jefferson.

"Give me an update soon. And I'll have him meet up with you to pick up that broken step. You can meet him outside the community somewhere. I'll have him text you soon to set up a time."

"I keep my phone on silent so I might not respond right away, but that sounds good."

Liv hung up and started walking back to the house, crunching twigs and dead leaves under her feet. In a perfect world, when things happened the way they should, she wondered if Isaac would marry Anna and she would marry Jefferson. It made sense and it was logical.

But would they be happy?

Liv knew deep down that even though Jefferson would be a good match for her, she'd never really love him.

*

Liv waited until one in the morning, when everyone in the community would be asleep. She put on a dress just in case anyone saw her because she didn't want to be caught in normal clothes.

She made sure her weapon was secure then crept out of the Mast house. She ran across the field to the Sullivans' house, carrying a small flashlight, shivering a little in the chilly night air. She went to the door that led to the basement, and luckily, it was unlocked.

Liv let herself in silently and tiptoed down the few steps until she reached the basement. Pointing her flashlight in every direction, she searched for whoever wrote *help*. Or maybe there was a secret door? There was no way she'd ever find it in one night by herself. But she had to try.

"Hello? Anyone in here?" she whispered, but there was no answer.

She searched for almost an hour. She felt along every wall and looked under every box that might be hiding something.

Nothing was here. Either whoever had been down here had escaped or Samuel had moved them to another location.

Then she made one wrong move. She turned and her elbow knocked over a metal box that clattered onto the concrete with a loud crash.

She froze, wincing as footsteps thundered upstairs.

"Who is down there?" a man hollered from the second floor.

Samuel!

Before he could make it downstairs, she darted up the basement steps and sprinted across the yard to the Masts' property, then leaned against the wooden wall of the house. Trying to catch her breath, she heard something. Shattering glass. What was that? It was coming from Isaac's house.

She ran down the lane until she reached Isaac's house.

Someone was smashing Isaac's buggy, bashing in the sides and shattering the windows with a bat. Olivia sprinted towards the vandal, but he saw her and started running away, dropping the bat in the process.

Was it the same weapon that had been used to knock Isaac out?

She ran faster and tried to catch up with the vandal, but he slipped away into the night like a phantom, leaving Liv bewildered and out of breath.

Giving up, she stopped and rested her hands on her knees. That guy was incredibly fast. Usually she was able to chase down a perp and pin him to the ground.

She turned back and picked up the bat, using the edge of her skirt as a makeshift glove so she wouldn't get her own prints on it. Jefferson could pick it up as evidence and send it to the lab where they'd try to get prints off of it and examine it to see if it matched the splinters found in Isaac's head injury.

Isaac rushed out of his house in a frenzy, his hair sticking up. He stared at the buggy and blurted, "What happened? What are you doing here?" No hint of accusation laced his words, only genuine concern.

"I know this looks bad, but I just saw a man bashing in your buggy with this bat. I tried to run after him, but he saw me and dropped this."

Now she really looked like a suspect.

"It's okay, Liv. I know. I saw the guy out the window. He vandalized my buggy?"

She breathed a sigh of relief. He believed her. "Yes. I didn't see his face. Did you?"

"No. It was too dark. Oh well, it doesn't matter."

"It doesn't matter?" She tried to hold back the shock in her voice, tried to stop words of argument from spilling from her mouth.

"Yes. I don't need to know who he was. Vengeance is the Lord's," Isaac said calmly, looking up into the starry sky. "Besides, it's just a buggy. The community will help me. It can be replaced."

An Amish man having his buggy vandalized was comparable to someone vandalizing her car, but she would be furious while the Amish would hardly react, turning the other cheek. She would want justice, but Isaac was willing to forgive and forget.

She gripped the bat so tight her knuckles turned white. She bit back another argument, knowing she was supposedly Amish now so she had to act like it.

"You're right. Mind if I keep this?" she asked, shoving all remaining thoughts of disagreement aside.

"Uh…sure, that's fine. Why?"

"I like baseball," she lied. *Baseball? Seriously?* She had never watched a game in her life.

"What were you doing out here anyway?"

"Just…taking a walk. Couldn't sleep."

"Okay. Well, we should get back to bed. Thanks for trying to help, even though you shouldn't have. It could have been dangerous."

Worry lined his voice.

I can handle it. "Sorry. I wasn't really thinking. Good night."

"Good night, Liv."

She walked back to the Mast house deep in thought. Samuel couldn't have run all the way to Isaac's after he heard her in the cellar. She hadn't seen him behind her, so he hadn't chased her, and she would have seen him run to Isaac's house through the open field. She was positive it was his voice she had heard shouting upstairs. Who else could it have been? He was the only man who lived there.

If Samuel hadn't vandalized the buggy and tampered with Uncle Gideon's staircase, who had?

Chapter Nine

At some point deep into the night, Olivia must have finally fallen asleep after coming back from Isaac's house, still wearing her dress.

She sat up in bed, listening. Something had woken her up. A gunshot.

Only one thought resounded in her head—*Isaac.*

Adrenaline pumping, she threw on her boots and shoved her gun into her jacket pocket, rushing out of the house quietly. She ran towards Isaac's house, flashlight in hand, hair flapping wildly.

Liv stood outside Isaac's house for a moment and listened. Silence. Then she heard rustling, followed by footsteps toward the door. She reached for her weapon in her pocket.

Isaac stepped outside. "What are you doing now?" he asked groggily.

"Same as you. Did you hear that? Was that a gunshot? I thought maybe you were hurt…"

"*Jah,* I heard it. But it didn't happen here. I'm okay." He smiled at her with appreciation. "Thanks for checking on me, though."

"Well, what are we standing around here for? Let's go see what happened." She cocked her head towards the other houses.

"Okay. Hold on a second." He put on some shoes and a jacket. "Let's go."

*

"Did you come here first?" Isaac asked as they ran toward the other houses, listening for someone crying or calls for help.

"Yeah. I thought maybe the person who injured you might have come back."

She was always the first on the scene whenever something dangerous happened. Why did she feel as though she had to investigate everything? Even as a child, Liv had always been a risk-taker, from climbing the tallest tree to pranking people. He smiled at the memories of her sneaking a toad into the teacher's desk, which even some of the boys had been too chicken to do. Or the time she had bet Isaac she could climb a tree higher than him, and she had won.

She had not changed much. It made her even more interesting.

Suddenly a cry pierced the night air. Liv looked up at him with coppery-brown eyes that shone in the moonlight. "Where did that come from?"

"It sounded like the bishop's house."

They ran up onto the white porch and knocked on the door. "Mrs. Johnson? It's Isaac."

"Isaac? Help!" called a voice between sobs.

They walked in to see the bishop's wife kneeling beside her husband, who lay on the floor in a circle of blood, a small bullet hole in his forehead.

Isaac's mind went back to when his grandmother had died several years ago. She, on the other hand, had died of old age peacefully in her sleep while this man had been murdered violently in his own home, with so much life ahead of him that he could have lived. And his poor wife and daughter... Poor little Jill. Now her father was gone, all because of a heartless killer.

It was utterly sickening.

The first time Isaac had seen the effects of death was when little Ava Sullivan, Jake's younger sister, had drowned when they were all children. Ava's brothers—Jake, Samuel, and Ian—and Isaac were supposed to be watching her swim in the pond, but the four friends had been so preoccupied with their games...

He would never forget the horrible accident. His gut wrenched at the memory of seeing his three friends weeping after they realized their younger sister had passed away, just like how Mrs. Johnson was sobbing now.

Ever since Ava had died, Jake Sullivan had been different, and his entire family was never the same. Jake's parents Diana and Bill Sullivan fought often, and their marriage had been clearly crumbling, but they stayed together. There was no such thing as Amish divorce.

Jake's older brother Ian had left the community as soon as he was old enough, probably overcome with grief and guilt, though no one spoke of him again because he was shunned for it. Over the years, Jake and his other brother Samuel became completely different people as they grew from boys into men—antisocial, unfeeling, and sometimes even callous.

Then Jake married Liv. Had Jake's heart turned so cold and cruel because of his younger sister's death and his brother being shunned for leaving? He had lost half his family, and he could see how it had also affected his parents' marriage. He must have felt an indescribable amount of grief and guilt.

Maybe that was why he had treated Liv the way he had, not that it was an excuse at all.

Death changed everything.

The Lord gives and takes away. Tears stung his eyes at the sight of the dead bishop. His heart went out to Mrs. Johnson and Jill.

"Isaac, are you okay?" Liv asked, pulling him from his memories.

"Yes, I'm fine. This is all so terrible. I was just lost in my own thoughts."

A second murder. When would it end?

At times like this, Isaac knew the Lord had a plan, but it was still so hard.

"What happened, Mrs. Johnson?" Liv asked, looking around. She began walking slowly around the room as if looking for something. "Where is Jill?"

"Mrs. Baker took Jill to her house so she wouldn't see her father like this." She gestured toward the body and wiped away a tear. "We were sleeping and there was a knock on the door, so he went to answer it. He said, 'Who is it?' and I heard a muffled reply. The hinges creaked—I assume he opened the door—then a moment later I heard the gunshot. I ran out here to find him dead." A new wave of sobs came, and Mrs. Johnson buried her face into her husband's cotton night shirt.

"Did you see who shot him?" Liv asked.

"No. He must have run off right away."

Liv looked out the windows. "So Bishop Johnson knew the person who killed him? Is that why he let him in?"

"He must have. He wouldn't have opened the door to a stranger in the middle of the night with what happened to Bill Sullivan recently."

"I'm so sorry, Mrs. Johnson. This is truly a horrific tragedy," Isaac said, though he knew no words would comfort her.

Mrs. Johnson only nodded, blowing her nose and wailing. Liv walked towards the bishop's body, then knelt down and picked up something small on the floor, using her skirt to cover her fingers, and inconspicuously tucked it into her pocket when Mrs. Johnson wasn't looking. What was she doing, snooping around like that?

Some of the neighbors ran up to the door and came inside, offering Mrs. Johnson condolences. Soon the room was full, and Isaac and Olivia listened to what people were saying.

"Who will be next?"

"Who is this vicious killer?"

"Should we involve the police now? How many more will die?"

"No. We do not need protection from the police. God will protect us."

Isaac watched Liv clenching her fists as she listened to the neighbors talk amongst themselves. She might be Amish now, but apparently she still didn't agree with their views on justice and not reporting crimes to the police. It might take her a while to accept, but he knew one day she would understand their ways completely again. Though sometimes he had to admit, it was extremely hard to forgive and forget and not seek justice.

Isaac put a hand on Liv's back, sensing it was time to go, and they walked into the night.

"What were you doing in there?" Isaac asked.

"What?" She shrugged her shoulders and raised her eyebrows.

"Snooping around, looking out the windows. And what did you pick up off the floor?"

"Nothing. What? I was just looking around the place. It's no big deal." Liv looked straight ahead as they walked back to Isaac's house. "Poor Mrs. Johnson and Jill."

Whatever she had picked up, she wasn't going to tell him. He didn't know what Liv was doing exactly, but he had a feeling she was trying to find out who the killer was.

And that was against the Amish way.

*

In the morning, Olivia called Branson from the woods near the Masts' house to inform him about the bishop's murder, the vandalized buggy, and why she looked in Samuel's basement.

"I have the 9mm casing from the murder weapon. I know that doesn't narrow it down very much," she said, disappointed that she couldn't find anything more.

"So this bishop let the shooter into the house?" Branson asked.

"Well, he opened the door, and his wife said he would only open the door to someone he knew after what happened to Bill Sullivan. The wife didn't hear who it was, though. But if the bishop knew the killer, the killer probably knew the people here don't lock their doors. He could have just let himself in."

"Hmm. Maybe he wanted to prove a point that they should lock their doors and not trust so easily. Do you think maybe this killer is a member of the community?" Branson asked.

"No. The Amish never murder. They aren't violent. Violence is against everything they are. It would be impossible." Liv shook her head even though Branson couldn't see her.

"What about your late husband?"

Liv narrowed her eyes. "He was the exception, and I had to kill him to save my life. I think his father abused him. His father didn't grow up here. He married into the church. So their family is not like the rest of the community, who are all good, pure-hearted people."

"Well, then, there could be another exception. You've been doing this long enough to know that killers are all kinds of people. What if it is someone the community knows well, like an outsider? Who do they see often outside their community?"

"It could possibly be a customer of one of their businesses. The Amish do a lot of work for *Englishers.* Or it could be someone who works for them, like a driver. But I don't see why one of them would have something against the community. Or it could be a friend..."

"I'll have Officer Martin come by today and pick up the bat, the step, and the 9mm casing. He can meet you around noon. Keep up the good work. Where is a good place for him to meet you? He'll take you somewhere and you can talk."

"There is an old, dilapidated blue shed at the end of the lane. Tell him I'll meet him there. I'll text him the address and directions."

She hung up and sighed, feeling like she wasn't getting anywhere. A yawn escaped her—she was exhausted. All she wanted to do was take a nap after barely sleeping last night. Seeing Jefferson today did not sound fun, especially with what was going on with Isaac. She was going to accept his offer of courtship soon, when the time was right.

Even though she was the one stabbing Isaac in the back, she felt as though a knife was going through her own heart. He was such a genuine man and really didn't deserve this, but in the end he would realize that she just wasn't the one for him.

She hoped she wouldn't hurt him too badly.

Jefferson texted her back a minute later and said he'd take her to a pizza place for lunch so they could catch up. It was far enough away that hopefully they wouldn't run in to anyone from the community there.

Just before noon she sneaked out of the house and walked to the end of the lane, taking a path through the woods so no one would see her carrying the baseball bat. She didn't want to be caught in her regular clothes in case she ran in to someone she knew, so she wore her dress.

She looked around to make sure no one was around, then approached the car. "Hey, Liv, you look—" Jefferson began. He tried to hold back a chuckle when he saw her in her old-fashioned clothes, but he obviously couldn't help himself. He burst into laughter.

She opened the passenger door, slid on to the front seat and smacked him on the arm playfully.

"You look great." He wiped a tear from his eye and grinned.

"Stop it! Now let's get out of here before someone sees me in your car."

Jefferson pulled out on to the street and drove to the restaurant. The waiter raised an eyebrow in confusion, probably wondering why an Amish woman was having lunch with an *Englisher.*

They sat down and she gave him the baseball bat, the step, and the shell in plastic bags.

"Thanks. I'll get these looked at for you. How's it going here?" Jefferson asked.

"Are you talking about the case or the personal stuff?" She sipped the glass of water the waiter gave her and squeezed a slice of lemon into it.

"The personal stuff. I know about the case and about last night." Jefferson picked up his menu.

"Well, a lot is happening. My former mother-in-law and brother-in-law hate me and are trying to make people think I could be the killer. I am technically Amish now, and I had to lie to an entire congregation about wanting to rejoin." Once again, guilt niggled at her, but she told herself she was just doing her job. "The community doesn't deserve any of this. They are the kindest, most innocent people. They shouldn't be lied to or targeted."

Then there was Isaac. She sighed.

"I hear an Amish man wants to marry you." He wiggled his eyebrows over the menu. "Is he hotter than me, in a sort of redneck way?"

Liv laughed, awkwardness settling over her. Jefferson was indeed very attractive, and he probably knew it, but he usually wasn't cocky about it. "He does not want to marry me. Yet. He only asked me to date him. And Branson told me to. You know, for my cover."

"Speaking of dating."

Oh no. "What's good here, you think?" She stuck her nose in her menu, hiding her face, pulse racing. Jefferson was a good friend, and she really cared about him, but she just couldn't picture dating him.

"Liv." He reached for her hand and held it tenderly. She waited, but she felt nothing except his fingers on hers and that terrible awkwardness. When Isaac touched her hand, her heart raced and a good feeling always filled her veins. But with Jefferson, she felt nothing. He was her partner, nothing more.

"I'll be straightforward. I've been meaning to ask you for a while. I was wondering if you'd go out with me. Maybe start a relationship outside of work." He looked at her expectantly. Seriously, he couldn't have asked her at a worse time.

She set down her menu and looked him in the eye, pulling her hand back. "I knew you'd ask me eventually. I'm sorry, Jefferson, but I like our relationship the way it is. We are co-workers and friends, and I don't want it to go beyond that. My career basically takes over my life, and I don't have time for anything else. It wouldn't be fair to you. Besides, this is a crazy time for me right now, being back where I grew up." She gave him an apologetic half-smile.

"I'm sorry. I understand though." She could tell he was disappointed even though he was trying not to frown. Pretending to have a sudden interest in the menu, he looked at it instead of her. "Branson said you left here on bad terms. He didn't say anything else, though."

"Yeah. It's been hard, remembering it all over again after I tried to forget for so long."

"Well, no matter what, you know I'm here for you if you need someone to talk to, okay?" He smiled at her.

"Okay. Thanks." She looked back on her menu, hoping things wouldn't be awkward between them from now on. She still really liked Jefferson as a partner, and she didn't want that to change. "Want to share a Hawaiian pizza?"

*

Liv returned to the Mast farm and helped Aunt Mary and Maria prepare dinner, then Isaac stopped by and invited Olivia over for dinner at his parents' house.

She really didn't want to lie to more people, but it would be nice to spend time with the Troyers again. When she had dated Isaac, she had practically lived there, spending time with Isaac and his family, since young dating Amish couples do not usually spend time alone.

Liv knocked on the door, then smoothed out her dress and her hair, hoping she looked okay. She had seen his family at church but had not had much time to really talk to them yet. She tried not to think about the fact that she was completely using their son and deceiving him in the worst way she could think of.

The door flung open and Hannah, Isaac's mother, stepped out onto the porch and hugged her. "It's so good to see you again! Come on in!"

Liv walked in and was greeted by all of Isaac's siblings—Jennifer, Kimberly, Simeon, and Jonah. They were all so much bigger than when she had left. The girls were busy setting the table, and Isaac walked in the house with Amos, his father.

"Hello, Liv! We are so glad to have you over tonight." Amos' voice boomed, and Isaac smiled at her, setting the butterflies aflutter in her stomach.

Then the guilt came once again, and she bit her lip. Tonight she decided she would forget all of that and try to have a good time.

They shared a delicious dinner followed by a board game, which the entire family played. Liv couldn't remember the last time she had laughed so much. More than once she caught Isaac staring at her with a foolish smile on his face. She blushed, feeling like a silly school girl again.

When Isaac offered to walk her home, dread seeped into her core. She was going to have to tell him she was ready for him to court her.

She wanted so badly to mean it.

"Thank you so much for dinner," Liv said on her way out the door. "I had a great time."

"Come back anytime!" Hannah called.

Isaac shut the door, and they stepped out into the peaceful night.

"Mind if I stop by my house and grab my jacket?" Isaac asked. "I didn't realize how chilly it would be. It was so nice out earlier."

"No, I don't mind." She zipped up her own jacket and walked a little closer beside him.

She wished the two voices in her head would stop fighting—the foolish voice who told herself to get closer to him, and the other sensible voice who kept reminding her how horrible a person she was and how hurt he was going to be. And that she was going to have to leave him behind all over again.

"So, remember when you asked me to tell you when I was ready for us to date?" she said quietly, wanting to kick herself.

"Yes." He glanced at her and grinned. His bruise was getting better, and she was glad the constant reminder of him almost getting seriously hurt, or worse, was fading.

"Well, I'm ready for you to ask me again."

He stopped and turned toward her. "In that case—Olivia Mast, would you please be my girlfriend?" He took her hand and gently kissed it, sending sparks up her arm as she let out a small sigh. He looked at her with those big green eyes that looked so dark and mysterious in the moonlight. He ran his hands down her arms and pulled her closer, and she let herself melt into his embrace, savoring the warmth and safety, and for a moment she forgot everything else.

Maybe she didn't want to be a detective anymore. Maybe she should stay here, marry him, and have a house full of children.

That was her inner foolish voice talking. The only way she'd be happy was to keep helping people get justice and help save lives. She couldn't do that here, in a place where people didn't believe in justice, the very thing she lived for.

The face from her last case appeared in her mind, the little girl named Miranda who had been kidnapped. Liv remembered how it had felt to help her out of that house where she had been held captive, out of that hole where she had been kept. The look in that child's eyes when she realized she was going home.

That was why Liv loved her job.

"Yes, I would love to be your girlfriend."

He bent down toward her, and she thought he was going to kiss her, but something stopped him and instead he only kissed her cheek. He had probably just reminded himself that dating Amish couples weren't supposed to kiss until their wedding day.

He took her hand and continued walking with a bounce in his step. "I am so happy right now."

Guilt ate at her.

They reached his house, and she waited by the door while he hurried inside. She watched a gas ceiling light go on inside as he searched for his jacket, knowing he never hung it up in the same place and hardly ever knew where it was.

"Liv?" His voice was thick with concern. "Come in here for a second."

She chewed on her lower lip. It wouldn't be proper for her to go inside, but no one was around.

"You sure?" she asked.

"You'll want to see this."

She threw open the door and stumbled in, walking to where he stood, looking at something on his kitchen table. All she saw was the square of white on the handmade table and the fear on Isaac's face.

He reached for it, but she stopped him. "Don't touch it!" she blurted out. She didn't want his fingerprints to get all over it so she could have it checked for the perp's fingerprints.

"Why not?"

"It could have poison on it," she said, making up something.

He drew back his hand quickly like he had touched a hot wood stove. She leaned closer to get a better look at the note.

I'm watching you. Tell your girlfriend to stop snooping around, or I will kill both of you.

*

Isaac's body went cold, despite Liv standing right next to him.

"What kind of person could do all of this?" he wondered aloud. "And why to us?"

"There are some messed up people in this world, Isaac. They do terrible, senseless things for no good reason."

"Maybe you should stop snooping around. If this guy isn't bluffing—"

"I'm not snooping!"

"Yes, you are! You're always asking questions, and you know I saw you take something, whatever it was, from the Johnsons'. It really isn't right, Liv, and you should let God handle it."

Her face turned red and she balled up her fists, then let out a deep breath. "This guy won't scare me."

Whatever she was up to, he knew Liv well enough that he wouldn't be able to talk her into stopping. The fact that someone was threatening his life was bad enough, but he would rather have this guy just kill him instead of threatening Liv, too. If Isaac was unable to protect her and she got hurt because of this killer, he didn't know how he would ever be able to live with himself.

The Amish were not supposed to protect themselves or kill in self-defense like she had when Jake had almost killed her. But she had done what she had to do, and it had saved her life.

He looked over at Liv as she stared at the note. She stood so close. A few fallen wisps of her caramel hair touched her collarbone, and he detected her vanilla scent. For a moment, he forgot all about the note.

Then he remembered again why they were in his house—alone. They had to leave before someone noticed. But he couldn't bring himself to step away, take his jacket, and walk her home. He wished they could stay there, sit at his table, and talk late into the evening, even if it meant breaking Amish rules.

As he looked at her again, gazed at her delicate features that defied her confident attitude that he loved so much, he realized he would act in self-defense to protect her. Even if he was shunned, it wouldn't matter, because he would do anything to keep her safe. He would not lose her again.

It was against everything he had ever been taught. But Liv was showing him a new facet of life. There were horrible people in this world, and one of them was preying on their peaceful, vulnerable little community.

He refused to just let this killer hurt the woman he loved. He would have to do something. His eyes traveled to his hunting rifle. He was an excellent shot as a hunter. Many Amish men were avid hunters. But that was all he was—a hunter. He had never considered using the rifle for any other purpose until now. Besides, that rifle was so big that he wouldn't be able to carry it around inconspicuously if he needed to.

Would he be able to do it? In the rush of a dangerous situation, would he be able to protect the one he loved? Would he be able to break one of the community's biggest rules?

He loved being Amish, and he loved God more than anything. He was the center of his life. He didn't want to disobey Him, but he was afraid for his life and for the lives of those he loved.

"What are you thinking about?" Liv asked, staring at him.

"Sorry. Nothing. Let's go." He grabbed his jacket and walked out the door.

*

Olivia had been so deep in thought about how she was going to grab the note without Isaac noticing that it had taken her a few minutes to realize that he was in a daze, staring off into space. She had no clue what he was thinking about, but he had an expression on his face that she had never seen before. Then he had just grabbed his coat and walked out, and that was when she stole the note, when his back was turned.

He would return home to find it missing, and she would lead him to believe that whoever had put it there had taken it back while he was walking her home.

Finally, she had some evidence. A threat. That was good. If she were lucky, the perp had been stupid enough to leave prints. She couldn't wait to call Captain Branson and have Jefferson pick it up.

Chapter Ten

After a sleepless night of deliberating and praying, Isaac pretended he was making a normal trip into town as he hitched up his horse and buggy the next morning. He was a horrible liar, so he was glad no one had asked him where he was going.

The buggy still had dented sides and a broken window, but it still worked. Isaac had an appointment made to have it repaired next week.

Finally, it was a warm day, and almost all the snow was gone. His horse, Rocket, plodded along. Tension began to twist inside him. How was he supposed to return home after this and act like nothing had changed? How would he hide his uneasiness as he constantly wondered when someone would realize what he had done?

He was breaking the rules. He had never really deliberately done that before. His whole life he had carefully, willingly obeyed the rules, but now he had to do what he thought was best.

I'm sorry, God. I have been taught my whole life that You don't want us to be violent or to kill another human being for any reason. And it is not that I don't trust You. But I hope You understand when I say this is something I have to do. I hope You forgive me, if this truly is wrong.

Wasn't there an example of self-defense in the Bible? As he tried to think of one, he could think of verses explaining how the human body is a temple of the Holy Spirit. Wouldn't God want the Amish to protect themselves from danger? When David killed Goliath, God had supported him. Wouldn't God support Isaac in protecting himself and those he loved?

Personally, this is what he thought was the right thing to do in this situation. He felt as though God would be all right with it, too. Even if it were a sin, he couldn't just stand by uselessly like he had last time and let Liv go unprotected. Not again.

He hitched his buggy up to the local outdoorsman store and barely noticed the strange looks he got from people walking down the street. They probably weren't from here and weren't used to seeing the Amish at a store. Maybe they thought the Amish were so antiquated that they simply made everything and that they never shopped. Sometimes the way outsiders viewed his people annoyed him. How people fit them all into a box of quaint perfection.

Well, the Amish were not perfect, and Isaac knew that. They were people, too, and they were flawed. Everyone seemed to think they lived perfect, sheltered lives and were immune to the evil of this world.

Now they had someone evil targeting their formerly peaceful community. Maybe nothing would ever be the same.

Isaac walked into the small store and strode right up to the gun counter. He had been here before several times for hunting gear, and he knew right where the gun counter was. He could not lie to himself. His eyes had curiously lingered on the sleek black handguns for too long more than once.

"How can I help you?" the clerk asked.

Isaac wore the most normal looking clothing he had. This clerk was new, so he probably had no idea Isaac was Amish.

"I need a handgun for self-protection. Nothing too fancy, not too big," Isaac explained.

"I've got this one." The clerk lifted an expensive looking pistol out from under the glass counter top.

"How much is it?" Isaac asked bluntly. The clerk showed him the price and it was more than he could afford, so he declined.

"Well, I do have this used Walther P99. It's great for self-protection." The clerk rested the black pistol in Isaac's flat, outstretched hands.

Isaac knew the gun was unloaded but he acted like it was loaded, not touching the trigger and keeping it pointed away from the clerk. It was a nice firearm. Not too heavy and not too big. He would easily be able to hide it.

"I'll take it. I'll need bullets too, please." He expected a wave of guilt to arise, but instead the guilt waned. A sense of peace settled over him. He'd made the right decision.

He reached into his pocket for the photo ID he had gotten during his *Rumspringa*. Since the Amish are against having their photo taken, they do not normally have photo IDs, but Isaac had always kept his hidden in a drawer in his house. He felt as though he might need it someday.

Looked like he was right.

He drove back home, almost feeling cocky. If this guy came back for him or Liv, he wouldn't expect an armed Amish man. It was simply unheard of.

After taking care of his horse and buggy, he loaded the gun. Then he heard a painful scream. What was happening now, in broad daylight? He threw on a jacket, hid the weapon inside the waist of his pants, and ran toward the scream. He hoped it wasn't Liv or one of their families.

Please God, protect them. And give me courage.

He ran down the lane toward the sounds of the cries. Smoke rose in the distance. Was that Sid Hoffman's place?

He turned and ran down the lane Sid lived on, passing trees that blocked his view, then skidded to a stop. Flames ravaged Sid's barn.

Who would set a barn on fire in the middle of the day?

Someone either very stupid, very bold, or very stealthy. Perhaps all three.

Isaac looked around for the arsonist, but he knew the guy would be long gone by now. Instead, he ran up to Mrs. Johnson, who had probably been the one who had screamed.

"Has someone called the fire department?" Isaac demanded.

"Yes! Sid is now." Mrs. Johnson wiped tears with her sleeve. "How could someone do this to us? When will they stop?"

Isaac considered his options. There was no way they would be able to put out a fire that size. There were no animals in sight. They had to still be in there.

Isaac ran into the burning barn, ignoring Mrs. Johnson screaming for him to stop, ignoring the sudden fear rising in his chest. He coughed in the thick smoke and looked around frantically. Only one side of the barn was burning, so he ran to the other side and let out

Sid's pig, goats, and horses. His eyes stung, but he worked quickly, and in a chaotic blur, the animals escaped and he stumbled out of the barn.

Liv came barreling around the corner and stopped when she saw Sid's barn, with Isaac running out of it. She stared at the fire, and Isaac swore he could see the burning flames reflecting in her eyes. She was clearly having a flashback of when her family had died.

Was this the same arsonist?

Liv covered her mouth with her hands as if to hold back a cry. She stared for a moment at the horrific scene, then turned away, shoulders shuddering. Isaac ran to her and put his arm around her.

"Sorry, I just remembered—" she whispered. "And you were in there. It made me think of—"

"Shh. I know, but everyone is okay." He gave her what he hoped was a comforting side hug. He wanted to wrap her in his arms and let her cry on his shoulder, but he couldn't with the bishop's widow standing there.

After a moment, she pulled herself together and hid her emotions well. Even though no one else noticed her pain, Isaac saw straight through her serious and calm charade.

"Hey, Liv. This might be bad timing, but the note was gone when I got home last night. Do you know what might have happened to it?"

Liv looked up at him with eyes that looked like they would spill over with tears at any moment. She shook her head. "I don't know. Maybe the criminal took it back?"

That meant the criminal had probably broken into his house again.

Isaac was so glad he had bought a gun. Hopefully, he could get in some target practice that afternoon or the next day. He'd be ready for the intruder next time.

Several more neighbors arrived, then the fire trucks came and put out as much of the fire as they could, but the barn was ruined. The community would come together to build Sid a new one.

That was one of Isaac's favorite parts about his people. During the worst times, they helped each other without fail.

After the firefighters left, Isaac and Liv wandered around, looking at the smoking remains of the barn without getting too close.

"This is terrible," Isaac muttered, knowing words could not describe the vicious crimes this culprit was committing against them.

Liv only nodded, looking carefully at the rubble as if searching for a clue.

As they were leaving, Isaac saw something black on the ground, and he reached down and picked it up. It was an Amish man's black hat, untouched by the fire. Sid only wore straw hats. This wasn't his.

He looked on the inside for initials. Then he read:

S.S.

*

"Liv! Look."

Liv rushed over and took the hat from him, reading the letters. She looked up at him with determination in her eyes, a lock of brown hair falling onto her cheek.

"Samuel Sullivan," she whispered, her hands trembling a little as she held the hat in her fists.

What was going on here? There was much more to what seemed like random acts of violence. With the word 'help' she had seen written on the Sullivans' basement window, the two murders, Isaac's attack, the stairs, and now this, she wondered how it all connected.

It had to be more than one person. Who had smashed in the buggy? It couldn't have been Samuel. There was no way he could have run to Isaac's house that fast right after Liv had heard him in his house. Did he have an accomplice?

And she knew the Sullivans' family secrets had some part in all of this. That the family was hiding something; she just didn't know what.

But what did these crimes have to do with that? Would someone go this far just to keep someone else quiet? She would take the first chance she got to call Branson and update him about this.

*

"Liv! Time to get up!" Gideon's voice boomed up the stairway as Liv rolled over in her bed and groaned. This was one thing she did not miss about the Amish—getting up early in the morning.

Then the memories of Sid's barn burning down permeated her mind, conjuring up painful memories of when her own house had burned down all those years ago. She hid under her pillow like a child, hoping she could hide from it or block out the sounds of her family's screams. But they raged inside her mind like burning flames, along with the memory of seeing the arsonist's masked face. She saw the angry clown mask in her mind, shuddered when she recalled the way she had felt—so helpless and afraid as she watched everything she loved be destroyed. Would the memories ever fade with time? Would she ever stop having these disturbing flashbacks?

She had to lie to Isaac yesterday when she had told him she didn't know where the note was. Jefferson had picked it up yesterday to try to get prints off of it. She had felt a twinge of guilt, but she hoped in the end he would understand.

She smelled the scent of breakfast cooking, and more guilt stirred within her as she sat up, pushing thoughts of the fire from her mind. Aunt Mary had probably already been up for hours, and once again, Liv had not awoken in time to help. She threw off the blankets and pulled on her frock.

After a hearty breakfast of biscuits with meaty gravy and fruit, the Mast family piled into the buggy, loading it up with the pies, casseroles, and cakes they had made the day before. When they arrived at Sid's house, there were already dozens of people there milling about and setting up long tables that would soon be covered with food. Children played and ran around, mini black hats bobbing and colorful dresses flying, their laughter lighting up the morning.

Liv helped Aunt Mary and Maria unload the food onto the tables, and Isaac came up to her. His dark, wavy hair was mussed in an endearing way, and the way he smiled made her feel warm all over as if rays of sunlight wrapped around her. She wanted to reach out to grab his hand, feel his strong forearm, but that would be inappropriate. She could tell he thought similar things by the look he was giving her, and she smiled at him shyly.

"Good morning, Olivia. Beautiful day, isn't it?" he asked.

"Yes. There are already so many people here." She looked over at the men who were arranging lumber to begin building. The women would not work on any construction, but would instead serve the food and drinks to the workers. She, for one, would be useless when it came to building a barn. She would rather stick to solving crimes, or in this case, serving food, even if she couldn't cook.

"It's good to see so many people come together to help someone in need. That is one of my favorite things about our community, that we always help each other," Isaac said with a warm grin.

She couldn't help but grin back. It was amazing to see so many people drop everything, including their own never-ending work and chores, to come help Sid Hoffman. The man greeted everyone enthusiastically, hugging the men and thanking everyone for coming.

Liv couldn't imagine how he could be so happy after someone had deliberately set his barn on fire, almost killing all his livestock. How could these people forgive and move on so easily?

Well, she knew it wasn't easy, but they did it anyway.

"Good morning!" sounded a chipper voice behind them. Liv turned to see a glowing Anna flutter over to them. "Hi, Isaac." She batted her eyelashes. "How are you?"

"Fine, thanks." His cheerful mood immediately vanished, replaced by a frown. He kicked a pebble absentmindedly. What was he so upset about?

Oh no. He hadn't told her yet?

He probably hadn't told Anna that they were dating. A terrible, guilty feeling washed over Liv as she imagined how hurt Anna would be once she found out.

And Isaac was not doing a good job at hiding his emotions. "Anna, we need to talk." He turned and started walking, and Anna followed him like a lovesick puppy.

*

Isaac tried to swallow away the guilt and shame that bubbled up inside him as he and Anna walked a short distance away toward the edge of the woods, just far enough so their conversation would be out of earshot of the community. He stopped and glanced over at Liv.

"So, what did you want to talk about, Isaac?" Anna stepped closer to him once he stopped. Usually Isaac would enjoy the way the light filtered through the trees in the nearby woods—like the way morning sunlight passed through his linen curtains. The woods were like home to him, since he was a hunter. He was himself there. But now that was the last thing on his mind.

He felt totally out of his element.

"Anna, there is something I have to tell you." Uneasiness rocked him like the stormy ocean would toss a boat on its waves.

"My answer is yes!" she cried, gripping his arm dramatically. "Of course, finally, you're asking to court me. I was afraid I was going to have to ask you myself!"

Oh no.

He hung his head. He had completely misled her! Clearly this girl could not read body language. She missed him chewing his lip, crossing his arms over his chest, and pulling away from her grasp.

"Anna." His tone was a little firmer, just to get her attention. "I'm not asking to court you. I am courting Liv. That's what I wanted to tell you. I'm so sorry."

"What?" She backed away. "Why didn't you tell me first?"

"I was going to tell you right after I asked her, but with the fire and everything going on, it completely slipped my mind. I'm so sorry, Anna." It was no excuse, but he said it anyway.

He had the worse sense of timing ever. Why had he chosen to tell her this now?

"You led me on." Tears rimmed her eyes.

"I really did not mean to, Anna."

"How could you, Isaac?" When she looked up at him with her big, teary eyes, he felt like the biggest jerk in the world.

"Please forgive me, Anna," he pleaded.

She let out a sob, covered her mouth, and ran away.

*

Guilt bubbled up in Liv's stomach. Here she was, leading on the man of her dreams, as she watched Isaac dismiss a girl who was a great match for him.

Indeed, the two were great for each other. Isaac was the ideal Amish man while Anna was everything Liv was not. Anna could cook, sew, bake, and keep a house clean. She probably wanted lots of children, and she was polite to a fault.

Liv sighed. Poor Anna. The sweet girl did not deserve this. Liv watched as Anna covered her mouth with her hands in front of Isaac. She ran up the hill and vanished on the horizon, her dress flapping behind her. Liv's heart broke for her.

She must be so confused right now.

But soon Liv would be leaving, and Anna would learn that this had all been an act for Liv's cover. Then Anna and Isaac would probably date and get married. Maybe Liv would end up with Jefferson. It seemed like that would be the logical, practical outcome.

Isaac and Anna deserved each other. Isaac deserved a true, honest, sweet woman.

As Liv's mind spun with questions, she barely noticed Diana sneaking up behind her.

"What did he say to her?" Diana snapped after she watched Anna talk to Isaac and fly over the hill. "She's just an innocent girl. What did you make Isaac say to her? What did she ever do to you?"

Liv whipped around to look at her. "I didn't make him say anything."

Isaac walked toward her, frowning.

Diana looked back and forth between the two of them, and Liv wished Isaac had never come over here with Diana standing there.

"You two are courting now, aren't you?" Diana asked, anger like fire in her eyes.

"Yes, we are," Isaac answered cautiously.

"You must be happy now, Liv, since you think he is so much better than my son was," Diana spat, coming a little closer. Isaac's jaw clenched as if to keep him from saying something he'd regret to Diana.

He is twice the man Jake ever was.

Liv stayed silent, not giving voice to her true feelings.

"I bet you're glad you killed him," Diana seethed, and Liv noticed how gray her hair was, how cold her eyes were, how much older she looked now. Then the anger swelled up inside Liv, but she suppressed it. A true Amish woman would not usually talk back or be as cruel as Diana was being.

"You know," Diana said loudly, "it is peculiar that you arrived just after my husband's murder and now, since you have been here, the incidents keep growing worse and worse."

Several of the people within earshot turned to look at Diana. Liv felt like panicking, but she kept calm.

Isaac put his hands on his hips in defiance. "Liv did not commit any crime."

"I didn't say anything about her committing a crime. You did." Diana glared at Isaac and Liv then turned and walked away. Liv's eyes stung with tears of anger. People were looking at her—most of them with furrowed or raised brows. Their gazes focused on her, and for a moment she was reminded of Jesus, who saved the very people who accused Him wrongly. He loved them even still and ministered to them regardless. She knew she was nothing like Jesus, but she had to still serve all these people as best she could.

Isaac came close to her, gently touching her arm. "Are you okay?"

"I just want to go home," she whimpered and wished everyone would stop looking at her, making her squirm. Her stomach churned with uneasiness. She just wanted to be alone, where she could be angry and cry and not have to pretend to be tough and unaffected.

"No, no. It's okay, Liv. You didn't commit those crimes, so don't worry about what others think of you. Come join the fun, and you'll forget about it in no time. Okay?"

She looked up into his eyes, which were beautiful in this light. The rim of dark green surrounding his irises fascinated her, soothed her. She loved that about his eyes. He was so gentle, and all she could think about was how much he deserved in life. He was so pure-hearted, the most genuine person she knew.

"Okay." She let him lead her to the building site and the tables, where several of the women greeted her.

"Diana was out of line when she said those things," Maria whispered into Liv's ear as she wrapped her in a hug.

Liv nodded, tears threatening again. But she willed them away, wishing she could turn off her emotions with a switch.

Never let your emotions interfere with your job.

Aunt Mary sidled up next to her and draped her arm around Liv's shoulders, squeezing and offering assurance. "No one believed her, anyway."

Liv doubted that.

Isaac's mother, Hannah, smiled at her warmly and nodded. "Just come help us, and you'll feel better before you know it."

And she did. They served the men drinks, and at lunchtime she sat with the women as the men ate, then they cleaned up after them before eating themselves, because there was not enough room for everyone to eat at once. The amount of food was astonishing, and there were lots of leftovers—vegetables, taco casseroles, soups, breads, shoofly pies, brownies, platters of cheese and deer sausage—all typical Amish foods in Unity. They'd be eating leftovers for the next few days for sure.

During the times when there was no food-associated work to be done like serving or doing dishes, Liv smiled when Hannah, Maria, Aunt Mary and some of the other women pulled out colorful quilts to stitch.

"You all never quit!" She laughed, and Aunt Mary grinned.

"We like to keep busy. Want to try?" She offered out her needle.

"No, thanks." Liv shook her head. "I'll only hurt myself or ruin your beautiful quilt."

Aunt Mary shrugged and began her sewing, and Liv watched in fascination as their needles looped up and down, back and forth, their skillful hands requiring no sewing machine, knowing exactly where to place every stitch. This community was like a quilt, each square of a person unique with its own color and pattern, stitched together by love and unity. She felt a little jealous of their creativity. She would never be able to create something so intricate.

She loved that this simple life they lived was centered on family and friendships and faith, cutting out everything that was unimportant to make more room for what really mattered. She wanted to somehow apply that to her own life and wished more people would.

At the end of the day, Liv walked home with her relatives, feeling so good to be a part of something that helped someone so much. But the shadow of the newly built barn was as dark gray as the sadness and worry that still lingered inside her, threatening to grow darker and darker.

*

Liv couldn't sleep that night, tormented by the memories of

people's accusing looks. Did they believe she was the criminal? If only they knew she was the detective investigating the crimes.

Liv tossed and turned for hours, then finally clamped a hand on her .45. If she couldn't sleep, she might as well take a walk and try to find some clues while no one would see her.

She put on a dress and shoes, placed the firearm in her holster, clipped her badge onto it, and looked out the window.

Farms and fields spread out over the vast land, the moonlight casting sleepy shadows on the lovely scenery. It was all so serene and peaceful, and it should have remained untainted by this world's evil.

But evil had wormed its way in. It always found a way in. Liv only hoped she would be able to conquer it.

There! Something moved near Isaac's house!

That perp will be sorry now. She anxiously hoped she'd be able to either get a look at him or catch him.

Not waiting a second longer, she grabbed her flashlight, dashing out of the house.

She ran to Isaac's house.

Please don't let me be too late!

She slowed down as she reached his property. The front was empty, so she ran around to the back. There, trying to quietly open Isaac's door was a large, burly man. The moonlight outlined his silhouette, and Liv immediately sprang into action.

For a moment excitement rose within her. Maybe she would see his face! Then she saw the ski mask on his head and her heart sank. She had to rip off that mask.

Challenge accepted.

She pulled the gun out of her holster, feeling the cool metal against her skin, and sprinted toward the intruder, hoping to sneak up on him. But he must have heard her, because he took one look at her and darted away in the direction of the woods.

She ran even faster, trying to catch up. Her lungs and legs burned as she sprinted, but it was no use. He tore off through the fields, surprising Liv at how quickly his legs carried his large body. She slowed down, defeated, as she watched him disappear into the dark tree line. Who was this guy, some type of Olympic athlete?

She kicked the ground in rage. He got away again! If it was even the same man.

She bent over, resting her hands on her knees, trying to catch her breath, feeling like she was getting nowhere with this case. She couldn't even catch up to the perp on foot. She desperately wished for more detectives to come work on this case, but she knew it was out of the question, as likely to work as building a snowman in Jamaica.

Somehow, she would have to arrest this guy on her own. She turned around to go check on Isaac, and a few minutes later was relieved to find he was safe.

At least one thing had gone right that night.

*

On Sunday morning, the birds woke Liv before any of her relatives did. The morning sunlight peered through the simple white curtains, and Liv stretched.

Isaac had been fine when she had checked on him the night before.

Since the man hadn't even gotten inside, Isaac had slept through the entire ordeal. He didn't even know she'd been there.

Liv went downstairs in time to help Aunt Mary and Maria make pancakes.

"Good morning!" Maria piped from her place at the stove.

"Oh, good morning. Want some help?"

"Sure. You can set the table and then help me cook these." Aunt Mary smiled at Olivia. She turned and stirred blueberries in her batter.

Liv went to the cabinets and set out the plates and forks and cups as Maria hummed while cutting up some fruit. Gideon came inside and they ate, then he read from the Bible. Liv actually listened, admiring Abraham's faith when God asked him to sacrifice his son. At the last moment, when Abraham was about to kill his own child, God stopped him. How had he had such faith? He trusted God with what was most precious to him.

Could she trust God to work this out somehow? To help her somehow catch the criminal, then go back to her life without hurting everyone she loved? Could they somehow understand?

God, I don't see how this will work out, but I'm going to trust You. Or at least I will try.

Gideon closed the weathered Bible and prayed aloud. Then they got in the buggy and drove to church.

Green was finally coloring the fields that spread across the community. Liv relished the sounds of the birds singing, the cows mooing, and the sight of horses nudging each other with their soft noses. The world was coming alive in Unity after a long winter. But

Liv felt as though winter had taken permanent residence in her heart. She longed for it to thaw and be joyful like the world around her.

"It is so beautiful here," she murmured. She had loved growing up here.

"It's a wonderful place to live most of the time," Maria remarked. "And to raise children. They can play outside without you having to worry about their safety or getting hit by a car. There's so much for them to learn here. You want children, right?"

Children? Ha. That was the last thing on Liv's mind. Her job overtook her life. She knew it would never leave time to properly raise children. "Of course. Lots of children." She smiled, hoping her cousin wouldn't see through her thin grin of a mask.

They filed into the church, greeting the other women, and Liv quickly took her seat. The church elders had voted in a new bishop, Bishop Byler. He was a kind, elderly man with a long gray beard who often wore a black hat. Liv had known him before she had left, and he had always seemed understanding and nonjudgmental. She watched him interact with the other men, laughing goodheartedly at something one of the men said.

As she fidgeted on the hard bench she sat on, waiting for the service to begin and twirling the ribbon on her *kapp* with her fingers, she thought about how everything in her life had happened the way it had for a reason.

If she had not killed Jake, she wouldn't have become a detective. Then she wouldn't have helped countless victims. Now she stood up for herself and wasn't afraid to protect others.

Yes, everything did happen for a reason. Maybe God had had a plan for her life all along.

"Good morning," the bishop boomed, his deep voice resounding through the room. His smile lit up the church like a child's laughter, and Liv relaxed a little. This would all work out. Somehow.

They began with singing. Olivia let her gaze wander to Samuel, then Diana, who were both glaring at her, narrowing their eyes as if silently threatening her.

Well, they had no idea who they were dealing with.

Chapter Eleven

After church, when they arrived back home for a day of rest, Olivia crept downstairs to get her cell phone from where it was charging. Then she ran off into the woods and called Branson.

"Hey, Liv. Got an update for me?" he asked, chewing something. "Oh, and we got the fingerprint results back for the note, the step, the casing, and the bat. We didn't get anything useful. This guy is smart enough to wear gloves."

"Great," she grumbled. Another dead end. "Well, last night a man tried to sneak into Isaac Troyer's house. He wore a mask, so I tried to sneak up on him, but he saw me and got away. I think it was the same guy who left the note, unless he has a partner."

"He was right there and you let him get away?" Branson retorted. "Come on, Liv, get your head in the game! What happened? You usually can catch a perp."

"I know, and I'm sorry." Remorse sunk in. "But you should have seen this guy run. Even though he was tall and big, he ran like an athlete. He outran me easily. I had nothing on him. I had no chance."

"Well, I hope you get a second chance." He bit into something again. She pictured him sitting at his big desk, a typical salami sandwich on his belly, crumbs falling as usual.

"I just really wish I could have some help here."

"No can do. You know we'd lose the people's trust, and then we'd get nowhere. You've got this, Liv. I believe in you." She detected a hint of sarcasm in his voice.

"Thanks for the vote of confidence."

"But seriously, I do believe you can do this. That's why I sent you. Look, just call me when you have a real update. Okay? And, you know, on second thought, if things don't start progressing, I might just have to send in more detectives. Maybe Jefferson. It might be our only option."

"I understand, Captain."

"Yeah. Later, Liv."

She hung up, disappointed in herself. She wanted to progress further into her investigation, but it was so hard working alone. She was used to working with Jefferson. If he came here, the people would become even more suspicious, then she'd have to work against them. Thanks to Diana, some of them already thought she was the killer. If she brought a friend in, they might think he was an accomplice. Or they would realize he was a detective and not reveal any more information about the murders.

And then the killer would probably realize Jefferson wasn't Amish, but that he was a detective, and possibly lash out in anger because he had told Liv to stop snooping around.

No, she had to do this on her own.

*

The man liked the way darkness covered the farmland like a shroud as he crept along the sides of houses, shying away from the revealing moonlight like a cockroach running when a light is turned on.

Darkness made him feel safe, and he didn't want to be caught. And he wouldn't be. He was smarter and faster than all of them.

Especially Olivia, who had tried to chase him down when he had attempted to break into the Troyer boy's house. What had she been doing out there in the middle of the night anyway? Snooping around again?

That Olivia Mast. That foolish detective. She thought she had him fooled into thinking she was an Amish woman instead of a cop. Ha!

He shook his head. She'd pay for the sins she had committed. That he would make sure of. He would hate to hurt her. She was so beautiful, and soon she would be his, but she still needed to pay.

He approached the Johnsons' house gingerly, first trying the front door where he had entered when he had shot the stupid bishop who had let him right in. Some people were just too naïve for their own good.

It was locked. No surprise. He didn't blame Mrs. Johnson for locking her door now that her husband had been murdered. But this was no obstacle for him. He easily picked the lock.

He crept through the kitchen, then past Mrs. Johnson's bedroom. He peered through the doorway and watched the older woman sleep, so unaware that her daughter was about to leave her to be with him. She would probably wake up in the morning and panic, but maybe she would eventually realize this was for the best. That Jill belonged with him, not her.

He shook his head at the oblivious sleeping form and tiptoed into Jill's room.

The moonlight illuminated the blonde hair around her angelic face like a halo. The little girl looked so peaceful in her bed, and for several moments the man stood in her doorway and watched her sleep, her chest rising up and down to the rhythm of her dreams. Perhaps she was dreaming about him. Though she had not seen his face, maybe in some other celestial world they had met before and her soul remembered.

He stepped toward her, pulled the bottle of chloroform from his pocket, and dampened his cloth with it. Then he clamped it over her nose and mouth.

Her brown eyes popped open, and she struggled. She thrashed and tried to kick the blankets off her, her small fists pushing against him, futile as feathers against his burly arm.

"It's all right, Ava. You're safe now. I'll keep you safe," he whispered.

Her fighting slowed, and her body went limp. Her lovely eyes closed, and she slipped back into unconsciousness.

She was his Ava, and it was time for him to take her to be with him, like a knight whisking a princess away to a castle. Then maybe the voices in his head would stop, the bad memories would cease. Maybe for once he would know what peace was.

He picked up her small body and carried her in his arms gently, smiling at the way her face rested against his chest. He would never let anyone hurt her again. Never.

He carried her out of the house and into the night, toward his safe place that waited for her.

As for that detective, he had had enough of her meddling and snooping around. It was time to scare her with more than just a note; then maybe she would back off.

*

Something had jolted Liv awake. She bolted out of bed, clutched her weapon, and peered out the window. Had she heard something?

There. A noise outside. Was someone trying to break into the house?

Not on her watch.

She dashed out her bedroom door and flew silently down the stairs. She stopped in the kitchen and listened for any movement within the house. Or had the noise come from outside? Perhaps she had heard someone trying to open a window or pick a lock on a door. It was as silent as a morgue in the house. She carefully opened the front door, hoping it wouldn't creak, and listened outside. The night seemed still, except for the staccato song of the crickets and the soft whooshing of passing cars from beyond the end of the lane. Maybe she was being paranoid.

Or not. Something caught her eye, something around the side of the house. She raised her pistol and stepped quietly down the porch steps, making her way around the corner of the house. As she followed the danger, her pulse quickened, yet anticipation rose within her. Maybe she would catch the killer tonight.

When she came around the side of the house, no one was there. She looked around the other side of the house, and there was nothing. She stood absolutely still, listening to the sounds of the night.

A bush rustled near the edge of the woods. Maybe it was a squirrel, but she had to be sure. The perp could be long gone by now. She approached the bush gingerly, gun raised, along with the hairs on the back of her neck. The bush shook again. Something was definitely there. Or someone.

"Police! Come out now with your hands up," she commanded.

The bush next to that one rustled, and now the movement was closer to her. A cat shrieked and lunged out, chasing some kind of small rodent into the night. It happened so fast, she couldn't even tell what kind of rodent it was.

She lowered her pistol, sighing, finally relaxing a little. The stupid cat had probably knocked one of Mary's flower pots over on the porch and woke her up. She was overreacting, over paranoid, jumping at every little noise. She was about to turn back towards the house when a large hand clamped a damp, sweet smelling cloth over her mouth. Chloroform.

Panic shot through her as she kicked and punched the attacker, then grated the slide of her weapon over his knuckles, trying to hurt him enough to let go, but he wore gloves. She tried to bite the gloved hands, but it was no use. He felt huge, easily overpowering her. She held her breath, knowing once she inhaled, she would become unconscious.

Don't breathe, don't breathe in! she told herself as her lungs burned. She remembered how Jefferson had once remarked that if someone held their breath when someone was trying to knock them out with chloroform, then pretended to become unconscious, it might give them the break they needed to escape. It sounded like a good idea.

She fought and flailed and twisted in his bulky arms, then let herself go limp, closing her eyes, still holding the gun loosely in her hand. The man supported her weight easily, then set her down on the ground gently. She opened her eyes so slightly that he wouldn't notice, trying to see his face, but it was hidden by a ski mask.

"Finally, we are together," he crooned in a deep voice, sending chills slithering over her body. "I've waited so long to be with you."

Finally? Waited so long? What was he talking about? Her mind screamed the questions, but she remained motionless.

"Now I will take you away so we can be together forever. You, me, and her."

No way. Not ever. She knew once she let him move her, she might not survive. Before he could react, she swung her handgun up and whacked him in the head as hard as she could.

He let out a string of curses and staggered back. She had been hoping to knock him out, but she must not have hit him hard enough. Now that there were a few feet in between them, she aimed her gun at him.

"Freeze. Move and I will shoot."

He hesitated for only a second, then dashed into the woods. She ran after him, unable to shoot in the black of the night. In the darkness, she couldn't see him, but she could hear the sound of twigs snapping as he ran. She would never hit him if she fired.

"No!" she shouted. He was right there! He was like a ghost, vanishing into thin air, and lightning fast. It was almost inhuman. How was she supposed to catch someone like that?

But Branson had picked her to come here because he knew she was capable. At some point the perp would mess up, and when he did, she'd be ready.

As she sulked back to the house and slipped back into her room, the man's words reverberated through her mind. What had he meant by finally being with her and waiting so long? And what other woman had he been referring to when he had said, "You, me, and her?"

She didn't know, but she had to stop him before he harmed anyone else.

He might not realize she was an undercover police detective yet, but he might figure it out soon. He may have heard her announce who she was to the cat. Besides, why else would an Amish woman have a gun?

*

The next morning, Liv attacked the kitchen floor with a sponge like it was a criminal while Aunt Mary washed the breakfast dishes.

"Thanks for that. You know, no matter how many times I clean that floor, it always just gets dirty again soon after. Sometimes I think, why wash it at all?" Aunt Mary laughed.

"Sounds like a plan to me." Liv chuckled and scrubbed with even more determination. The least she could do for this family was help them with cleaning.

"Did you hear?" Maria busted through the door, running into the kitchen with her boots still on.

"Hey! I'm washing the floor! Get your boots off," Liv ordered with a laugh, waving her dripping sponge, then saw the look on Maria's face. Suddenly the floor seemed unimportant. "What's wrong?"

"Jill Johnson has been kidnapped! Poor Mrs. Johnson. The murder of her husband is bad enough, but now that her daughter is gone missing we are concerned she might have a nervous breakdown." Maria sighed and collapsed into a chair at the table.

"No! That's horrible! When did it happen?" Liv stood up. The floor would have to wait.

"Last night."

"Did Mrs. Johnson see anything?"

"Nothing. She woke up and Jill was gone."

"That is terrible!" Aunt Mary exclaimed.

So caught up in their own conversation, Maria and Aunt Mary didn't even seem to notice when Liv slipped out of the house. She ran toward the shanty and pulled her phone out of her holster, dialing Branson's number. It rang once before he picked up.

"Yeah," he muttered.

"It's Liv. Remember Bishop Johnson, the man who was shot in his home? Well, his daughter Jill went missing last night."

"What? Now we're talking about a kidnapping? Did you question the mother?"

"Listen, my cousin told me Mrs. Johnson didn't hear or see a thing, and I believe her. Besides, if I go question her, she'll just get suspicious."

"Okay, so what's your plan?"

"I really think Samuel Sullivan took her. His initials were on a hat we found at the scene of Sid Hoffman's barn fire, and then there was the word 'help' written on his window. He might be trying to frame me. I'd like your permission to tell Isaac the truth about me so I can get him to help me solve this. He was best friends with Samuel as a child, and he knows him a lot better than I do. Maybe he knows something helpful."

"Won't Isaac hate you for lying to him?"

"That's the thing. The Amish don't hold grudges, and they always forgive. He might be mad at first, but he'll get over it and then he'll help me, hopefully. Even if he just gave me some information it would help."

"He better not tell anyone anything," Branson warned.

"Don't worry. He's trustworthy."

The captain sighed. "Okay, I guess it's a better alternative than bringing in Jefferson. Besides, Officer Martin is busy on another case. Just make sure Troyer doesn't blow your cover."

"He won't," she assured him.

"Fine. Call me later."

She hung up and went to find Isaac. It was Saturday, so he'd be home.

She jogged over to his house and knocked on the door. He opened it and smiled, then his smile fell. "What's the matter, Liv?"

Was she that bad at hiding her feelings? Did her fear show through that easily? He did know her well.

When she didn't answer, he pulled her inside. He had been cleaning, she could see. The broom was out, along with cleaning supplies and rags.

"Liv, what is it?" he asked her again, pulling out a chair for her.

She eased into it, trying to choose her words.

"Did you know Jill was kidnapped last night?"

"No! That's horrible," he cried, plopping into another chair. "Her mother must be worried sick."

Liv nodded. "Isaac, I think I know who kidnapped Jill."

Isaac gave her a skeptical sideways look. "What?"

"There's something I've got to tell you. You're not going to like it, but right now I need you to put aside your emotions because I desperately need your help. We only have a certain amount of time left." With every passing hour, Jill's chance of survival decreased. After twenty-four hours, the chances of finding Jill alive would be small.

He leaned forward. "Liv, you can tell me anything."

He had no idea.

She dove right in. "I'm a detective. I work at Covert Police Detectives Unit." She closed her eyes, anticipation and regret seeping through her. *Please, God, don't let him hate me.*

"What?" He leaned back into the chair and laughed. "Is this some kind of joke?"

"No. I was sent here to investigate Bill Sullivan's murder and the other crimes that have occurred. I go undercover to investigate crimes." She pulled up her skirt and Isaac flinched, looking away. She knew he would think it was improper to see her knee, but it only took a second for her to grab her badge and weapon and toss them onto the table.

She expected him to run from the gun, but he stayed put, staring at the glinting badge.

"You're serious," he murmured. "You lied to me this whole time? About us?" His voice rose. His face turned red, and he got up and started pacing.

"Listen, Isaac, I dated you as part of my cover, yes. But that doesn't mean I don't actually care about you," she pleaded. "Please, you have to believe me."

"It doesn't even matter because you're going to leave again, aren't you? After this case is solved?" He whipped around. "You're going to leave me again?"

She weighed her options, biting her lip. She had to get him to help her, which meant she would have to lie to him again to keep him interested, to prevent him from dumping her. "No. I actually am considering joining the faith for good after this assignment is over."

"Really, Liv?" he asked gently, coming back to his chair. He grabbed her hand. "That's wonderful."

"I mean, I'd have to learn a lot more about God again. I'd like to have a better relationship with Him." That much was not a lie. She had indeed forgotten much of what she had learned about God growing up, and she missed how close she had been to Him.

"I'll help you, I promise." Isaac ran his thumb over her hand so tenderly she sighed. His touch sent invisible sparks up her arm once more.

"But still, you lied to me." He turned away and stood up again. She knew he was confused right now, so she gave him space. "But I guess I understand. It just really hurts, that's all."

"I know. But really, Isaac, I need you to help me. I need information on Samuel Sullivan. You were friends with him when you were children. I need you to tell me anything helpful that you know about him. Okay? It could help us find Jill. It could save her life."

"All right. Could I pray first? I just need to clear my head or I won't be able to think straight. Just for a few minutes." He was already brushing his fingers over the doorknob.

Every second was precious, but she figured he deserved a minute after the shock she had just put him through. "Okay, but hurry back. We have work to do."

He slipped out, and she found a pen and paper and began to write. But after a few minutes, she threw down the pen. Her list of suspects was short.

Where was he? Couldn't he forget his pain for five minutes to help her save Jill?

She got up and stomped outside.

"Isaac, come back!" she shouted into the woods. She knew he was in there. That was his favorite place to be.

*

"Oh, God, please tell me what to do."

Isaac crashed through the trees, crunching fallen twigs and dead leaves carelessly as he walked, distracted by his own grief.

"What if she leaves again? I just don't think I could bear to see her leave a second time. I want to spend the rest of my life with her."

She was going to leave. He just knew it. Liv wouldn't ever want to live here.

He collapsed onto the ground and cried, pain wracking his chest, gripping him tighter with every passing moment like talons clutching a small, helpless animal. He wiped his tears and looked up at the sky through the tree branches. The thought of losing her again was unbearable. And he had the feeling she was lying about staying.

"Why did You bring her back into my life just to take her away again?" he demanded. "It doesn't make sense."

His tears eventually slowed, and as he wiped them on his sleeve he looked around at the beauty surrounding him. The woods usually comforted him, but today they weren't enough. He sat still and listened to the community that lived here, just as complex as his own. The skittering squirrels, the birds in the trees, and the bugs crawling on the ground. The woods teemed with life and sounds that might go unnoticed to anyone else, but Isaac was aware of every movement and noise.

Then he heard Liv calling his name.

She was right, they didn't have time for this. He pulled himself together and walked back toward his home, kicking himself for delaying their search. Poor Jill must be terrified, and here he was wallowing in his own trivial sadness.

Jill needed his help, and he would do whatever he could to help Liv find her.

He stepped out of the tree line and saw a dark, sinister figure creeping towards Liv as she called for him, completely unaware of the intruder.

"Liv!" he screamed, but it was too late.

*

Liv growled with annoyance. Yes, she would be mad too if someone had lied to her like that, but hadn't Isaac had enough time?

"Isaac!" she shouted again.

Isaac came out of the woods and screamed her name. Why did he sound so panicked?

A large gloved hand clamped over her mouth, cutting off her scream. Her eyes widened in panic, her heart rate tripling.

Choking back her fear, ignoring her insides twisting with terror, she brought up her elbow and smashed it in his face as hard as she could, impacting his nose.

While he was recovering, he stumbled a little, and she took the opportunity to turn and hit him with a right hook, then she kicked him as hard as she could. He staggered again, and she tried to get her firearm out of its holster.

Her skirt got caught in the holster and suddenly the masked man was back on her. He put her in a choke hold and knocked her down. Her head hit the ground with a thud.

Pain exploded in her skull, rattling her mind as he pinned her down. The world spun, and she fought to remain conscious.

Please, God, don't let him kill me. Her thoughts blurred and ran together. Where was Isaac when she needed him? Not that he'd be much use right now anyway. He didn't even believe in self-defense.

"I told you to stay away, girl!" the attacker seethed, gripping her shoulders. She could feel his hot breath on her face. "Stop snooping around!" He sounded as if he was purposely trying to make his voice

165

sound different. Since it sounded so deep and hoarse, he sure didn't sound like Samuel, but some people were good at disguising their voices.

"Liv!" Isaac shouted as he approached.

She felt for her .45 and loosened it out of the holster while the man still held her down.

Finally.

As the perp was distracted by Isaac's voice, Liv gripped her pistol and started to lift it, but he knocked the gun out of her hand.

While she lunged for the gun and stood, he bolted toward the trees.

Chapter Twelve

"Stop or I will shoot!" Liv shouted.

When the criminal kept running, she fired at him. The gunfire echoed off the tree line through the fields, but she missed as he disappeared into the woods.

As Isaac ran, he fixed his gaze on her, admiring her bravery. She stood firm, feet planted, skirt billowing around her, *kapp* skewed sideways. Dirt smudged her determined face and her clothes, but she didn't seem to notice.

She was dangerous with that weapon, but for some reason that made her extremely attractive.

And he loved her even more.

Again, he hated himself for not being there for her. He had been carrying his gun, and maybe he could have shot at the perp to protect Liv. But would he have had the courage to do it—one of the things the Amish were most against?

Was he willing to be shunned in order to protect the woman he loved?

He knew without a doubt that he was. He would have done it. But he hadn't had the chance because of his silly emotions.

I will never make that mistake again.

*

"Liv! Are you okay?" Isaac asked as he ran over.

"I'm fine. Come on, let's get inside."

Yanking on Isaac's wrist, she tugged on him firmly, practically dragging him to the other side of the house and through the front door. Isaac shut it and pushed his couch in front of it because his door didn't have a lock.

Liv went to the living room window and peeked out. "This guy is like a ghost. He is so fast I can't even get close to him, and I'm pretty fast. He leaves no evidence. He just sneaks around, killing at will. He's trying to scare me so I'll stop investigating."

"Is it working?" Isaac gave her a sideways glance.

"No. Of course not," she retorted.

Isaac wrapped her in his arms so tight she feared he'd fracture one of her ribs. "I'm so sorry I wasn't there. I heard you call me, but I was just being selfish. I should have come back—"

"It's okay, Isaac. Really, don't worry about it," she muttered into his chest. "Now stop your blubbering and go over there so we can watch for him out the windows."

He stepped back and moved to peek out the front kitchen window, and Liv stood by the edge of the back window in the living room.

"What did he do to you?" Isaac asked, not taking his eyes off the kitchen window.

"Well, first he politely asked me how I was doing, then he asked me if I like knitting."

He laughed despite his remorse. "I can't believe I wasn't there to protect you."

"Come on, Isaac. We both know you wouldn't have had the heart to hurt him."

"Actually…" He reached into the side of his belt and pulled out his Walther P99 handgun. "I got this the other day."

Liv glanced at the gun but then resumed watching outside. "What? You, Isaac Troyer, have a gun? What's next? You'll start smoking and swearing, too?"

He chuckled. "No, I won't do those things. I just wanted to protect you and myself, and anyone else who might be in trouble. I've been practicing my shooting. Just don't tell anyone I'm carrying, okay?"

She sighed. "Under the circumstances, I understand why you're doing this. But I'm shocked, Isaac."

"I hate to see you hurt like this… again."

"Hey, at least it was some deranged guy and not my husband this time. It's part of the job. It happens. I'll be fine. Besides, I fought back. You should have seen the other guy."

He couldn't see her face well from this angle, but he guessed she was smiling mischievously. "Next time, I promise I will protect you. I'd rather die than lose you again, Liv."

He looked at her from across the room, and she knew she'd get lost in his gaze if she didn't look away. Her eyes darted back to the living room window.

"I'll tell you what I know about Samuel." Isaac grabbed a pencil and paper and set it on the kitchen counter so he could still see out the window above the sink.

As they continued their conversation, they didn't stop looking out the windows. Liv said, "Let's make a list of suspects. Write down

Diana and Samuel. They were all I could think of. Can you think of anyone else? We are pretty sure it is someone this town knows, because Bishop Johnson opened the door to let in whoever shot him. Bishop Johnson must have known his murderer."

Isaac looked off into the fields, thinking. "I can't think of anyone who would have something against all of the people who have been attacked here. What do all of the victims have in common?"

"Nothing really, except that they are Amish. This is a long shot, but do you think a customer of one of the community's businesses might be angry?"

"Angry enough to kill and commit arson, murder, and kidnapping? No. We always make things right with our customers. No, this is something personal." Isaac scratched his head.

"Well, all I can think of is the Sullivans. I know that family has a lot of secrets. I'm just not sure what they are, except that Jake was abusive and possibly Bill. But why were they? What made them that way?"

"Well, we do know that Bill used to be an *Englisher* and that he married Diana, so he became Amish. But I heard that he regretted his decision, hating this way of life, and blamed her. If he was abusive, that's most likely why Jake was abusive," Isaac said softly. "I think Bill Sullivan started a vicious cycle."

"That means Samuel and Diana are probably victims of domestic violence. Not only did he most likely physically abuse them, but he probably verbally abused them, blaming them for everything. Sometimes that alone can make someone go off the deep end, depending on the person. Do you think it might be enough to make them do these things? Maybe they are taking their revenge on the community for not stopping the abuse. Did people know it was happening? Did the bishop know? Did you know? Or Sid Hoffman?" Liv asked.

"I had no idea until recently. I was young back then. I didn't notice anything wrong. But I wonder if the bishop knew." Isaac smacked his hand on the counter. "Maybe Samuel or Diana killed him for revenge!"

"Now, that makes sense. But why hurt you? Why kidnap Jill? What did the two of you ever do to them?" Liv shook her head, her mind boggled.

"Well, we don't know what happened to me the night I was attacked. I could have witnessed something. As for Jill… You know, Samuel had a little sister named Ava. Remember? She drowned when she was five at that pond in the woods."

"Oh, yes. That was such a long time ago. It's all coming together now. Either Samuel or Diana must have killed Bishop Johnson for not stopping the abuse, then they must have kidnapped Jill to replace Ava." Liv was filled with excitement, finally feeling like she was getting somewhere. "It is starting to make sense now! I knew you could help me figure this out. Now, help me think of where he could be keeping Jill. Then I'll call Captain Branson."

"Okay. There was this old abandoned cabin we used to play in when we were kids. Samuel called it his safe place, probably because he went there to get away from his father. He loved to go there. I'm the only one who even knows about it now that Jake is dead. We never told our parents or anyone. It was our secret place. I know where it is, too. Think he might keep her in a place like that?" Hope filled his eyes, and he looked at her with anticipation, awaiting her answer.

"Absolutely." Liv nodded. "Sounds like a perfect place for a sociopath to stash a kidnapped child. I'll call Branson right now to get some backup so we can go look for her there."

She got her phone out from her holster, dialed Branson's number and looked out the window during the entire call.

"Branson here."

"It's Liv. I think we know where Jill is. Isaac told me about a place where he used to play with Samuel when he was a child, an old abandoned cabin in the woods no one else knows about. We think he is keeping her there, and Isaac can lead us to it."

"Excellent news. Want me to send a team over?"

"Yes, but keep it quiet. Have them meet us near the woods, away from the homes so no one suspects anything or sees Isaac and me with them. There is a spot near the woods where nobody will see CPDU's vehicles. I can text you directions if you want."

"Sure. I'll send them on their way right now. Tell Isaac thank you," Branson said.

"Yes, Captain."

Liv hung up the phone and texted Branson the directions for the meeting place.

"We have to go out there again. Let's be careful, of course," Liv told Isaac.

He nodded. Liv looked out the windows again. When she saw it was clear, she stepped outside, hiding her pistol under a fold in her skirt. Isaac came out after a moment. Nothing happened. If the attacker was still watching them, it seemed like now was not the time to attack them again, or maybe he really was gone.

"Let's go." She sprinted with Isaac toward the tree line where they would meet the team from CPDU, all the way to the other side of the community, away from the Amish homes.

Several minutes later, the police cars pulled in and parked near the edge of the woods.

When they all exited their cars, they gathered around Liv and Isaac. She made quick work of explaining the plan. "Everyone, this is Isaac Troyer. If you remember, he was hit in the head and attacked the night Bill Sullivan was murdered. He knew Samuel Sullivan as a child and was the one who thought of the abandoned cabin in the woods. He is going to lead us to it. Samuel Sullivan is considered armed and dangerous. We suspect he is the one who has committed all the crimes here." She turned toward Isaac. "All right, lead the way."

"Follow me." He started trekking through the woods. The team was rather quiet as they made their way through the woods, though they did keep snapping branches left and right. After about ten minutes, Isaac stopped.

"The cabin is right over that hill," Isaac told them.

"Okay." The lead officer took over and barked directions to the group. "You two, go around the back. You two go in on each side. The rest of us will go through the front door. Let's surround the place. The

kidnapper could be inside with the victim. Now, quietly, let's move."
He gave the signal and the officers crept up the hill, then surrounded
the cabin noiselessly. Isaac stood back at a distance, but looked like he
wanted to be a part of the action. Liv hung back a little too, since she
wasn't wearing a bullet proof vest like the other police officers.

The lead officer held up three fingers, then two, then one, and then
he kicked the door down. "Police! Put your hands up!" he shouted,
expecting Samuel to be inside. The other police stormed in like knights
invading a castle, shouting and searching.

Liv couldn't wait one second longer. She ran into the cabin after
them, her gun held up, sweeping the room, searching for Jill and
Samuel. The cabin was falling apart, completely in shambles. Broken
furniture lined the walls, and the cracked windows were covered in
grime. She expected a mouse to run by at any moment.

"He's not here!" the lead officer shouted. That was when Liv saw
Jill tied to a bed in a cobweb-laden corner of the cabin. Several of the
officers were already cutting the ropes to set her free.

Was Jill unconscious or was she… *No!*

Liv darted towards her and felt her pulse on her neck.

She was alive, but groggy. Probably drugged so she wouldn't move
or call for help. How could a person do this to an innocent child? How
could someone be so evil?

One of the officers picked her up and carried her out after all the
ropes were off. Liv followed closely behind. She wanted to question
her as soon as she woke up.

Every officer seemed to be talking at once, calling CPDU to give them updates. Isaac stood outside the cabin, watching everything going on with fascination.

"This is all so amazing," he murmured. "You all rescued her."

Liv told him, "You're the one who led us here. We couldn't have done it without you, Isaac. Thank you."

He shrugged shyly. "Just glad I could help. You know, I would really like to learn more about what you do. It's all so interesting to me."

"It's not really as glamorous as it looks, but we all love our jobs. I'll teach you about it if you want," Liv said.

*

Jill was taken to the hospital, and Liv and Isaac followed the ambulance in one of the patrol cars. They waited in the hallway for her to wake up. Liv wanted to be the first one to talk to her. Mrs. Johnson had been informed that Jill was found, and she was on her way. Finally, the nurse came out to talk to them.

"Jill is going to be all right. She was drugged with chloroform. She needs to stay here overnight so we can flush the drug out of her system. She's a little groggy, but you can go in and talk to her now." Liv was still in her Amish clothing, so the nurse had no idea she was a detective.

Liv and Isaac went into the room, and Liv pulled up a chair and sat down next to Jill.

"Hi, Jill. My name is Olivia. You've seen me before, right? And you know Isaac."

Jill nodded. "*Ja*, I've known Isaac my whole life, and I've seen you at church. Where's my mom?"

"She's on her way. Listen, I just want to ask you a few questions. Do you remember anything that happened last night or today? Do you know who took you from your house?"

"No, I didn't see his face. He had a black mask on that covered his whole head. I woke up, and he was standing over me. He put something wet on my mouth." Jill shrank back under the covers, trembling at the memory.

Liv hated to do this to her, but she needed the information. "I know this is hard for you, Jill, but you're doing a great job remembering. Did he say anything to you? Anything you remember would help."

"*Ja*, he said something. He called me Ava. And he told me I'd be safe with him." She pulled the covers up to her chin. "Is that bad man going to come find me here?"

Ava? It was Samuel! Now she was sure.

"No, no, Jill. You really are safe. That bad guy is going to jail. He won't come near you ever again." Liv squeezed the little girl's hand.

*

Samuel was taken into CPDU for questioning, and finally Liv felt like she could relax. That night, after they were dropped off at Unity, Liv walked with Isaac back to his house.

"Thank you so much for all your help, today," she said as they approached his porch.

"I'm really glad I could help."

Contentment washed over her as she watched him walk in to his house, the moonlight covering the landscape in a soft glow.

"Good night!" she called after him.

"Good night." He shut the door.

Liv walked back to the farm and sat on the Masts' porch, leaning back in a wooden chair, staring up at the stars after a long day. She didn't even need to wear a jacket. The night was warm, and the sky was cloudless. She marveled at the millions of stars. The sky was so clear, and they were easy to see here unlike in the city.

She looked out over the farmlands, hearing the soft neigh of a horse in the distance, the land peaceful and quiet. She smiled a little, thinking of how nice it must be to live here.

It just wasn't for her.

In the distance, near the Sullivans' house, a large dark figure moved swiftly through the night.

"What?" Liv muttered aloud. Samuel was in custody. Who was this? Was this his accomplice?

In two seconds she was off the porch and running toward the intruder, loaded gun in hand. He wouldn't get away this time! She was sure of it.

Adrenaline pumping through her, she sprinted across the fields until she reached the Sullivans' house. From behind some bushes, she watched the intruder creep inside like a slithering snake.

She darted up to the house. The door was open. Liv crept through silently, sneaking through the kitchen, then towards Diana's room. Her .45 was raised, ready to fire at any second. This time, she would shoot at him before letting him get away if she had to, now that Jill had been found.

The only person who was home now was Diana. She knew that was who the intruder was after. He had killed Bill, and now he was probably after his wife. Liv tiptoed toward Diana's room, and her heart pounded so loud she wondered if the perp could hear it.

Liv halted. The intruder stood in Diana's doorway. His large frame seemed to take up almost the entire space, eclipsing the moonlight coming into Diana's bedroom window. He was clutching a white cloth in his hand. Had he already drugged Diana?

Something glinted in his hand. A knife!

She had to do something. She could shoot him, but she was afraid she might hit Diana, who was right behind him on the bed.

"Police! Put your hands up!" she commanded, her voice shaking. The man froze. "Turn slowly. Drop the knife. Now! Do it!"

He slowly turned, but gripped the knife even tighter than before. Again, he wore the mask. This was the same man she had seen attack her, smash Isaac's buggy, and try to break into Isaac's house.

The police had arrested the wrong man, unless Samuel had a twin.

"Couldn't stay away, could you?" he seethed.

Why wasn't Diana waking up? He had to have already drugged her with the chloroform.

"I'll make you regret this, all the meddling you do. I told you to stay away over and over. Jake was right about you. You just don't listen, do you? No wonder he treated you the way he did." The man took a step closer to her, his white teeth flashing in the dim, milky light seeping through the windows. How had he known Jake? His voice and his words made her shiver.

Did she personally know this man? If so, why didn't she recognize his voice?

"If you had been married to me, I would have probably just killed you," he taunted. Anger rose within her at the way he talked about Jake and how he had treated her. "Especially since you loved that Troyer boy all along."

That's not true! She focused on the gun in her shaking hands.

She stepped back, but he came even closer. He was still directly between her and Diana. What if she missed and hit Diana or the bullet went through him and hit her? "Stay back. And drop your weapon now!"

"Or what, you'll shoot me? Risk killing Diana, or me, when you could get information from me? You would really do that?" He glowered at her.

He was right. He overcame her in an instant, swiftly swiping the pistol out of her hands in one quick blur of movement. He held her close to him, so close that she could smell his cologne, a woodsy scent that otherwise would have been pleasant but now disgusted her. She wriggled and tried to twist out of his grasp, but he only held onto her tighter.

"You weren't ready for that, were you, little police lady?"

Liv had been trained for years on how to never let someone take her weapon. She had been successful until she encountered this man who was incredibly fast.

He wrapped his arm around her neck and held the gun to her head.

"You scream and she dies," he growled into her ear. Liv looked at

Diana's unmoving form in the bed. For all she knew she could have already been dead. "You probably would be happy if she died. You should be, after the way she treated you. She basically told you it was your fault. She said she didn't believe you. Even when you showed her the bruise on your shoulder that day as she made you a pot of tea."

Disbelief and a sick feeling washed over her. He spun her around to face him. "How did you know about that? I never talk about that. You would have had to—"

"Have been there? I was, darling. I've been there, watching you, many times in the past. I know some of your little secrets, your quirks. I know the TV shows you like to watch late at night. I know you eat peanut butter cup ice cream at two in the morning. You can't cook, so you buy tons of microwavable dinners. And I know you came into this house seeking help and advice from your mother-in-law, and she said you deserved Jake's abuse because you couldn't cook or sew or be like any other of the Amish wives in town. You knew she was hiding something, didn't you? You knew Bill was abusive too, and he was hurting Diana, just like Jake hurt you. And that's why she covered up Jake's abuse. Because she didn't want to ruin her family's reputation. Because she didn't want to admit the truth."

Liv swallowed the bile rising in her throat, nausea stirring in her stomach. He had been watching her? And she had never even noticed? She, a cop, should have known. She should have noticed a noise, a shadow, a movement…something.

"You know, I was going to take Diana tonight. But I'm glad you crashed the party, gorgeous. So, on second thought, since you're here…"

In confusion, she looked up to see his arm raising. He placed the damp cloth over her mouth and nose so quickly, even before she had a chance to remember to hold her breath.

She couldn't fight it. She felt as light as a cloud, and her knees gave out from under her, her surroundings fading to black.

Chapter Thirteen

Liv groaned, her head foggy for some reason.

Realization and memories of the masked man slammed into her. Her eyes snapped open to see a wooden, beat up floor from where she sat. Boots covered large feet in front of her, and Liv's eyes traveled up to peer into the face of her kidnapper. Finally, his mask was removed. A huge, muscular man in his late thirties stared back at her, his blond hair cut into a military high and tight. His cold, steely blue eyes bored into her face. Then she looked down at herself, trying to stand up and run, but she was tied to the chair she was sitting in with ropes.

No! She panicked, her heart rate speeding up. She tried to get free, but she was caught like a butterfly in a net. She hated this, hated being confined, feeling claustrophobic.

"Don't bother. Houdini himself couldn't have gotten out of those knots," he gloated and walked toward her as casually as if he was on a walk in the park. She noticed her cell phone on the table, the battery taken out so no one could track her. This man was smart. There was a Glock sitting beside it. Was that the weapon used to kill Bishop Johnson?

The man pulled Liv's gun out of his belt. Anger burned within her, boiling her blood at the sight of him handling her M&P Shield. That was *her* pistol, and now it was in a killer's hands!

"Why am I here? What do you want with me?"

"Well, for one thing, you just wouldn't quit trying to stop me. I couldn't have that, and even though I threatened you and your boyfriend, you ignored my requests. Second of all, you killed my brother. And that is unforgivable."

His brother? What, was this guy adopted? "What? I don't understand."

"Well, that's rude. You don't recognize me?" He leaned toward her and gripped her arm. She shrank back from his cold touch and his closeness, squirming. "Think far back."

Oh, my.... She took in a deep breath of realization, her eyes widening. "Ian Sullivan." The young man who had left the community years ago. Now that she thought of it, he was almost the same size as Samuel, only a little bigger. Much scarier. No wonder she had thought he was Samuel when she had seen him masked.

"Correct! In the flesh." He flipped his hands palms up. "You were young when I left, but still, I'm surprised you didn't remember me. I had a big crush on you back then, you know," he said coolly, walking around her.

She tried not to gag. He was several years older than her, and she must have been just a little kid at the time. What was wrong with this sociopath?

"Anyway, about you killing my brother. It really is time that you pay. You know, after I came home from my tours in Iraq and Afghanistan, I looked for you for months. Then, one day, I found you. I found out you work at CPDU. Found out you liked to go out to eat at that little Thai place on the corner. And I found your house." His gravelly voice grated her sanity. He turned to her, and those cold eyes gripped her like talons. "Look, see what I made for you?" He motioned toward the wall, and she turned her head.

There, covering the wall, were pictures of Liv. Photos of her eating at her favorite café, pictures of her at the laundromat, the bookstore, near CPDU, and walking on the street. There was a close-up of her face at the grocery store. He had to have been right near her to have taken such a close-up picture! How had she not noticed?

"This one is my favorite," he whispered, pointing to one in the middle. It was of her sitting on her couch watching TV. In her house!

He had been in her house? And she hadn't even realized it. Her breath caught in her throat, and her heart felt like it had dropped to the floor.

"Well, I do love this one, too," he murmured, and she looked where he was pointing. It was of her sleeping. "You look so peaceful, so serene. So beautiful."

He had been in her bedroom? Bile rose in her throat. The room spun, and she started breathing faster and faster as her heart rate doubled and lightheadedness crept in. She was having a panic attack.

He had been stalking her. And she had had no idea the entire time. How had she been so careless and oblivious?

He came toward her and caressed her face with his sandpapery fingers. She turned her head away as if he had slapped her. If she wasn't tied up, she would have gladly socked him in the face for that, but all she could do was sit there in disgust.

"I was going to kill you that night in your house, but I enjoyed watching you too much. You're a beautiful woman, Olivia, even after chopping all your long hair off. I see now why my brother married you. I wanted you to myself, but Jake told me he was going to marry you even before you dated Isaac Troyer. But then I left and forgot about you...until I got a call saying you had murdered my brother!" His voice raised an octave at the end, his face reddened, his fists clenched. For a moment, she was afraid he was going to hit her. She let out a breath of relief when he didn't.

"I didn't murder him!" she cried. "He was trying to choke me to death. The court said I only acted in self-defense."

"I don't care what the court says!" he retorted in rage. "You killed my brother, and that's all there is to it. And now, you're going to pay for what you did to him."

He turned to a small table at the front of the shack and picked up the knife he had been holding in the Sullivans' house. He ran his fingers up the side of the blade, smiling at her sinisterly.

Her stomach twisted with a sickening fear. No, it was something beyond fear. She was terrified, more terrified than she had ever been in her life, except for when her house had burned down with her family inside. Why was he dragging this out?

He glared at her. "You know what else? You took the little girl away, didn't you? You found her in that cabin where I was keeping her and took her." When she hesitated, he lunged toward her and screamed, "Didn't you?"

"No. Actually, that was the police." She spewed out the words.

Wait. She had something he wanted. Something that might keep her alive, maybe buy her some time or give her a way to escape.

"She was my Ava. She looks just like Ava looked when she was alive. She's about Jill's age when she drowned. The same blonde hair, the same innocent brown eyes." Ian got a faraway look on his face as he turned and looked out the window. "Ava drowned in that pond, right there." He moved, and she looked out the window to see a still pond, smooth as glass. "I come out here when I really miss her. Helps me feel better. But after a while, I missed her more than I could bear. I needed her back. I knew if I took her back I would stop hearing my father's voice in my head, constantly telling me it was my fault she drowned."

He turned to face her again. "I was supposed to be watching her that day. But I got distracted playing a game with my friends while she was swimming. Playing with Jake, Robert, and Isaac. Then, after a while I turned around to check on her, and she was gone. She died, and it was all my fault.

"My father blamed me every day after that. He never let me forget, not even for an hour. It was just too much, so I left. I joined the military, became a Navy SEAL, went overseas, then came here to look for you to get my revenge. Then I realized, maybe if I killed my father, his voice in my head would stop. So I shot him. But still, the voices didn't stop.

"Then I thought maybe if I killed the bishop, I'd feel better. After all, he should have done something about my father's abuse. He should have known there was something wrong, and he should have done something about it. He had to pay for what he did, so I shot him." He spoke matter-of-factly, showing no remorse for the murders he had committed. He stabbed the knife into the table top, making Liv jump.

"So…you believed you were serving them justice," she concluded.

"Definitely." He nodded.

He was so twisted! She understood he had been hurt, but that was no excuse to commit murder!

"I have one question," she said meekly.

"What?"

"Why did you attack Isaac Troyer the night you killed Bill?"

"What…? No, I didn't attack Isaac. I smashed in his buggy, because you love him, but I didn't attack him. I was going to, that night I tried to sneak into his house, but that was when you came along and shot at me." He growled and pulled the knife out of the wood.

"What about trying to run me off the road on my drive here? Was that you?"

"I was trying to prevent you from getting here and investigating, but it didn't work so well, did it? Not even when I threatened you that night."

"You could have killed us!" Liv snapped.

Ian shrugged unsympathetically. "But I didn't. I care too much about you to kill you."

Liv tried not to roll her eyes. "What about the note in Isaac's house?"

"Oh, yeah. That was me. I was trying to scare you into not snooping around anymore. But I guess you don't scare that easily."

"No, I don't," she retorted, then wished she hadn't. He came at her, holding the knife up.

"Oh, really? Let's see about that…" He brought the knife closer to her arm, and she asked him another question to distract him.

"What about the fire at Sid's house?"

He chuckled, then backed off, the boards of the shed creaking under his weight. She let out a breath, slowly, quietly, her heart slowing a little.

"Yeah, that was a good one. I got one of Samuel's hats from his house and put it there in the rubble, trying to make you think he was the one behind all this. And you fell for it!" He laughed, then touched his chin. "Besides, I like fire."

Fire? And when she had first arrived and he had threatened her from the woods, he had talked about her family dying there in the fire.

Liv's little sister had been the same age that Ava had been when she had drowned, and had had blonde hair. Would Ian's grief push him so far that he would burn down the house of a family who had a daughter the same age as his sister when she had died?

She wanted so desperately to ask him, but she knew she wouldn't be able to contain herself if he admitted to the crime, which could anger him and get her hurt. She pushed the question out of her mind to save for later.

She looked away. Yes, she had fallen for his tricks. "So, Samuel didn't do any of this? He didn't help you?"

"Nope. It was all me. I was just hoping you'd think it was him. I got you good, didn't I?" He smiled again, flashing those white teeth.

"Yeah. You got me good," she muttered.

"But now, you have to pay for all you did to me, especially taking Ava away from me. I mean, Jill. Look," he demanded, grabbing her chin and forcing her to look at the other wall, which was covered in more pictures.

Pictures of Jill Johnson.

"I love that little girl as if she were my own sister," he said softly, making disgust wash over her as her gaze wandered over the photos. There were images of Jill playing in the fields, helping her mother hang out laundry, riding in a buggy with her parents, sitting on her front porch swing with her father. There was a close up of her shopping at a store with her mother.

"You've been stalking her, too?" Liv cried, feeling even more disgusted than when she had found out she had been stalked. At least Liv knew how and was willing to protect herself. But Jill was as vulnerable as a wobbly foal. He could have easily killed her while he had her in that cabin, and Liv thanked God that he hadn't.

"Yes, for a long time. She is so much like Ava. She *is* Ava. I knew if I had her back, everything would be fine again. I'd be happy. But now I don't know where she is."

Liv swallowed the overwhelming guilt rising in her throat. She couldn't believe what she was about to say.

"I know where she is."

Ian whirled around. "Where? Tell me!"

If Liv could convince him to let her take him to Jill, it would give her a chance to call for help or escape. "Better than that, I can lead you to her. And I can get you close to her. You really think you'd have a chance of getting close to her once she sees your face? She'd scream for help the second she sees you!"

"Where is she?" he demanded, grabbing her arm again.

"The nearby hospital. I know what room she is in. She is protected by security, but Jill knows me and she likes me. They'll let me in, and if you dress like the Amish, they'll let you in with me." She hoped he would buy her bluff.

"If I dress that way, they might let me in alone."

"You don't want to risk that. For one thing, they won't recognize you as her friend. And you don't want to risk Jill screaming for help." She watched him think, pondering his options.

"Right. Okay, we leave now." He whipped out his knife again, and Liv flinched, fearing the worst. But all he did was cut off the ropes binding her to the chair.

He brought the knife up to her face, and she froze.

"You try anything, and I swear, I will kill you and Isaac. And your family. Or what's left of it. Are we clear?" Maniacal fire burned in his eyes.

She believed him. "Crystal."

He opened a box and pulled out an Amish man's shirt, pants, and hat. "I kept these from when I lived here, just in case I ever needed them. Good thing I did, even though they might be a bit small for me now." He lifted a small lavender dress out of the box. "This was Ava's. I will be glad to see it put to good use again." The way he smiled made her sick, but she stood up shakily, slowly, ready to do whatever it would take to save Jill's life and escape.

"Wait. There will be security guards. How do you expect to get her past them?" She watched his reaction, hoping she had stumped him, but he just gave her a smile that made her skin crawl.

"I can make a decoy version of her." He grabbed some clothes and blankets off the floor. Liv watched in horror as he fashioned what resembled a child's body out of the fabric and some rope. He put the Amish clothes on it. With the round cloth head covered by a *kapp,* and the rest of it covered in the frock, it looked like a giant cloth doll. But when Ian picked it up, rested it against his shoulder like a sleeping child and draped a blanket over it, Liv's stomach fell to the floor.

It looked like Ian was carrying a sleeping little Amish girl. Realization sunk into her like a poisonous fluid in her veins.

His plan might work after all. What had she been thinking, telling him where Jill was? Would the security guards realize what was happening and stop them?

If anything ever happened to Jill because of Liv leading this crazed maniac to her, she'd never forgive herself. She would do everything she could to protect that child, even if it meant risking her own life.

"Are we ready, dear?" He lifted one eyebrow.

She couldn't speak, and he didn't wait for an answer. He led her to his car in the woods behind the shack. He put her in the front seat with her hands still tied, then he quickly changed into his clothes behind some trees. He walked over to the car, and though his shirt was too tight around his bulky arms, he definitely looked like an innocent Amish man.

As they drove to the hospital, Liv thought of every possible way she could either escape with Jill, get someone's attention, or somehow get help. Maybe she could stab Ian with his own knife, causing a scene and injuring Ian long enough to give her the chance to tell someone she had been kidnapped. Maybe she could somehow slip someone a note. Or make a sign to show the security cameras.

Possibilities swam through her mind. They both stayed silent and listened to the radio as they drove. When they pulled into the parking lot, Liv felt sick as he cut the ropes that tied her hands.

"Let's go," he ordered, prodding her. He rested the decoy on his shoulder like a sleeping girl again and the draped a blanket over it. Liv got out of the car and walked with him toward the hospital, slowing down a little with each step. But each time Ian noticed, he pushed her forward.

They walked inside, got on the elevator and went up to the third floor. Liv spotted Jill's room. With every step, Liv's feet felt as though they were sinking further and further into cement. Ian grabbed her arm and all but dragged her to Jill's room.

The security guards stood watch by her door. Liv stared at them, begging them with her eyes to stop them. But they just looked at Ian and Liv's clothing and remained oblivious to the threat right in front of them. Ian nodded at them politely.

"Idiots." He whispered the insult as they entered the room. Jill was asleep on her bed.

"I'm sorry, but the patient should be resting right now," a passing nurse told them as she saw them walk in.

"We just drove a very long way and our driver had some car

trouble. We are friends of Jill's. She'll want to see us, and we'll only be a minute. Could you make an exception just this once?" Ian flashed her a deceivingly warm smile, using his charm to the max. "We will be quick."

"Well…" She bit her lip, looking at their quaint clothing just as the security guards had. Why would she expect them to do anything ill-natured? "All right. You can have a few minutes." She walked away.

As soon as the nurse was out of sight, Ian hurried to Jill's side.

"Oh, Ava," he cooed. "I missed you." He pulled the piece of cloth and the bottle of chloroform out of his pocket and raised it, putting it over her mouth. She woke up for a second then fell unconscious. Ian removed the clothing from the makeshift giant doll he had made, then stuffed the decoy under the bed.

As he was leaning over, Liv made a split-second decision. She lunged and grabbed the knife from out of his belt. Before she could even raise it, he was on her, whisking the blade out of her hands and thrusting it back into his belt, concealing it under his pants. He wrapped his burly hands around her throat.

"I told you not to try anything," he seethed, his rancid, hot breath on her face. Images of Jake trying to strangle her flooded her memory. She cringed, wriggling in his grasp, then he released her and whispered, "If you call for the guards or try anything else, I'll stab her right here and now."

Suddenly the nurse appeared at the doorway again, her short dark hair bobbing. Ian hid the Amish dress and *kapp* behind his back just in time. "Are you almost done in here?" she asked.

"Oh, yes." Ian grinned.

The nurse smiled. "Okay." Then her gaze fell on Liv. "Hey, weren't you here with another man named Isaac last time?"

Ian smoothly put his arm around her shoulder, but the nurse didn't see him pinch her skin, hard. She winced.

"Uh, yeah. That was my brother."

"Hmm… That's not what Jill told me. She said Isaac was your boyfriend." The nurse looked suspicious.

"Um, I mean this is my brother. Sorry. It was quite a trip here. I must be more tired than I realize." Liv lied as badly as she could. With Ian's arm around her like that, it should have been obvious that he wasn't her brother. She hoped the nurse would pick up on something, realizing something was wrong. An Amish woman would never date two men at once, and hopefully that was common enough knowledge for the nurse to realize that.

"Oh, I see. Where did the little girl go?"

"Well, my mom is here too, and they went to the bathroom together."

"Okay, then," the nurse said awkwardly. "Finish up in here, okay?" She left again.

Ian grabbed Liv and whirled her around. "Try a stunt like that again, and I will kill you and Jill. Got it?"

Liv nodded rapidly.

Ian whipped out the dress and blanket from behind him. He yanked the dress onto the unconscious, limp girl, right over her hospital gown. He put on the head covering.

"You really think that will work?" She hoped that it didn't with all her heart. They kept their voices down so the guards outside the door wouldn't hear.

"In case you hadn't noticed, no one has been paying attention to us except that nosy nurse. The woman at the desk hardly looked at us. The guards didn't blink. No one will think twice about an Amish couple leaving the hospital holding their sleeping child in their arms." Ian sounded annoyed as he finished putting on her dress. He unhooked Jill's IV, and Liv hoped that wouldn't hurt her.

Liv glanced at the doorway. But the guards didn't even bother looking their way.

"I better put this where you can't reach. Just in case you try something stupid again. And if you do try anything, I really will kill both of you." He took the knife from his belt and tucked it under his shirt. Then he picked up the child and carried her over his chest. Jill truly did look like she had fallen asleep in his arms and did not look much different from the decoy he had been carrying before, especially when he draped the blanket over her.

Oh, no, this maniac was right. No one would notice, would they? He was going to slip out of the hospital, kidnapping a child in plain sight.

"Ready to go, dear?" he said, walking out of the hospital room, putting an arm behind Liv to make her walk next to him. The guards didn't look at them twice as they walked by. Liv was about to give them a signal, but Ian looked at her and gave her a warning glance that only she noticed.

They went down the elevator and walked into the lobby. Jill looked so peaceful in Ian's arms, just as any daughter would look as she slept, safe in her father's hold. But inside Liv, a storm of turmoil and desperation raged, and she tried to show it to the people surrounding her without Ian seeing.

The woman at the desk didn't look up as they passed, though Liv desperately wished she would. Liv tried to give pleading, fearful looks to everyone who passed by, but no one seemed to care. They just walked along, smiling blankly, politely, not even noticing what was going on right under their noses. Why would they? There was no reason to suspect an Amish family of anything.

Ian had been right. No one even realized that they were witnessing a crime.

Ian put Jill in the backseat, buckling her as she remained unconscious. They got in the car and drove back to Unity, and the entire time Liv shook in fear, trembling at the thought of causing this innocent child to be back in the captivity of a sociopath. How could Liv buy more time? Someone at the hospital would notice them missing soon and come looking for them. Maybe Isaac knew about the shack, just like he had known about the cabin, and would tell the police.

But Isaac was probably already asleep for the night, and he might not even realize she was missing until morning. As for the hospital, she didn't know how long it would take them to realize Jill had been taken.

Please, God, send someone to rescue us. And if not, give me the strength to get us out of this situation safely.

"Here we are," Ian announced, throwing the car in park. "Well, looks like we'll be camping out here for the night. I'd offer you a bigger space, but *someone* already found my cabin hideout. It's no longer a safe place to stay."

Ian got out of the car and unbuckled Jill, carrying her into the shack. Liv knew she could run as his back was turned, but she knew he would hear her and shoot at her. Then Jill would be left alone with her kidnapper.

No. She would not save herself and leave Jill behind.

They went inside the shack where Ian rolled out a mat for Jill to sleep on, and he carefully set her on it. He tied up her hands and feet as she was still motionless, then he tied Liv back onto the chair. Great. Tied up again.

"Now go to sleep." Ian unrolled a sleeping bag for himself.

"Here? Like this?" she asked incredulously. How was she supposed to sleep tied to a wooden chair?

"I know you'll try running off, so I have no choice but to restrain you like that. Or, if you'd rather, we can share my sleeping bag."

"No thanks. I'm good." She wasn't sure if he was kidding or not. She'd rather sleep on the edge of a cliff than anywhere near him.

"Get some rest. We leave in the morning."

"Where? Where are we going?" Liv panicked. If he took them somewhere else, they might not ever be found. Why didn't he just kill her?

"Not sure yet. Just go to sleep." He lay down and closed his eyes.

Liv knew at that moment she wouldn't sleep one moment for the entire night. Overcome with worry, she trembled throughout the night, drifting in and out of a half-sleep. Her neck hurt and she was stiff, but that pain was nothing compared to the anxiety within her.

Please, God. Save us.

*

"Olivia?"

Liv heard a small voice calling her name and she opened her eyes. Morning sunshine was pouring in the small window, brightening the small shack. She looked down to see Jill waking up on her mat.

"Olivia, what's going on?" she asked, her eyes darting back and forth. She pushed herself up into a sitting position, her blonde hair mussed. "Why am I tied up again?"

How was she going to explain this? "Well—"

"Good morning, Ava. Did you sleep well?" Ian rummaged around the shack, putting things into a bag.

"My name isn't Ava. I told you that before." Jill shrank back into the corner of the shack. She stared at Ian wide-eyed, and Liv knew that even though Jill might not have seen Ian's face, the girl knew this was her kidnapper. She showed every sign of distress—rapid breathing, shifting eyes, covering herself with her arms, trying to get as far away from him as she could. But the child had nowhere to run, and Liv's heart broke for her.

"Why am I tied up?" the child repeated, trying to tug her hands free. "How did I get here?"

"Well, your friend Liv here told me where to find you, so we went and took you from the hospital. And now, we're leaving," he explained.

"No! Where are we going? I want to go home to my mom." She cried, her brown eyes filling with tears. She was actually handling this very well. If this had happened to Liv at that age, she would have had a panic attack. "Why did you take me?"

"Well, Ava, the truth is, we need each other. I need you more than your mom does, and I can keep you safer than she ever could and take better care of you. I've been watching you for a long time now, my dear. Look. See what I made for you?" He showed her the wall of pictures.

Jill stared up at the collage of herself, all the photos of her at home and even at school, or doing chores. She shook her head wildly. "No, no. We aren't supposed to be in pictures. It is considered vain."

"You had no idea I was taking these pictures, so don't worry. It's not your fault." Ian knelt down to her level. He touched her shoulder, but she wriggled away.

"Why did you take all those?" she asked, squirming.

"Because you are my sister, and I love you, and I wanted some pictures of you. Aren't they lovely?" He presented the collage as if it were a masterful work of art.

Jill looked at it skeptically, then she glanced at the other wall. "You took pictures of Olivia, too?"

"Yes. I've been watching her, too. Anyway," Ian continued, stuffing more things into a box. "We are going out of state. We leave now." He went to the wall with Liv's photos on it and began taking them down carefully, laying the photos in a box. Then he started taking down Jill's pictures.

"Where are we going?" Jill demanded. "Please, take me home!"

"I can't, Ava. We need to go somewhere where we can be a family. Here, no one understands the love we have for each other. If we go somewhere else, we can start over. Finally, we can be one happy family." Ian turned to Liv and looked at her in a sickening way. "What I said before about killing you if I were Jake, that wasn't true. I always knew that if I married you, you would have been much happier with me than you ever were with him. I promise, I will take better care of you, Olivia. I have lots of plans for you."

She wished her hands were free so she could plug her ears. With the way he looked at her, she almost wished he would just kill her now rather than carry out whatever plans he had for her.

*

Knock knock knock.

Isaac stirred in his bed and groggily opened his eyes. Was that someone knocking on his door?

Knock knock knock!

There it was, much louder this time. Oh, no! He must have overslept for work again. He had only done it once, and Gideon had been understanding, but he had promised himself he wouldn't do it again, and now he had. He passed a hand over his face and ran his fingers through his hair, then scrambled out of the bed and threw on a shirt. He hoped Gideon wouldn't be angry with him.

"Coming!" he shouted and ran for the door. He pulled it open to see a tired, worn Gideon standing on his porch.

"Oh, Gideon, I'm so sorry for oversleeping—"

"No, Isaac. That's not why I'm here."

Gideon looked older all of the sudden. Worry lined his face, aging him by a decade.

"Have you seen Liv?" Gideon asked.

"*Jah*, I saw her last night when she walked me home, after we visited Jill in the hospital." Then, like an avalanche, worry hit him. "Why, what's happened?"

"She never came home last night. We never heard her come in, and Mary is a light sleeper. When we woke up, we realized she was gone. And Mrs. Johnson just told me Jill was taken from the hospital and is now missing."

Liv! And poor little Jill. Isaac collapsed against the doorway, his knees giving out. His vision tunneled, and for a moment he was afraid he'd pass out. Gideon instantly reached out to support him.

"No! I should have walked Liv home last night. We thought she'd be safe now that Samuel was arrested!"

He would have done anything to protect her, even shooting the criminal if he had to, but he didn't say that in front of his boss, who didn't even have a gun for hunting.

"Wait, Samuel was arrested?" Gideon asked. When people didn't have cell phones, word didn't travel so fast.

"Yes… I guess you haven't heard what happened yet. I'll tell you more later."

"Liv could have been taken too," Gideon replied in an urgent tone.

That had to be what had happened. Liv was supposed to go to her house, and she wouldn't have left like this. "Let's go pray with the others."

"No, you go ahead. I need to get myself together here." Isaac motioned for him to go.

"All right." Gideon didn't argue. He hurried off.

Isaac retreated into his house and collapsed at the table, thinking. Samuel clearly was not the culprit. But his sister had been named Ava, and the man who kidnapped Jill had called her Ava. No one else had ever been named that here.

Then realization struck him like a speeding car. There had been one more son in the Sullivan family, a son who had been forgotten long ago when he had left the community. The sound of his name had died the day he had left. No one had spoken of him since, so it was like he had never existed, except in people's memories. Isaac still remembered his childhood friend.

Ian Sullivan. It had to be him.

Isaac remembered how Ava had drowned while Ian and Samuel were supposed to be watching her. The rumor was that Bill blamed Ian for Ava's death because he was the oldest, so that was why Ian had left.

And that was why he had kidnapped Jill and called her Ava. Jill resembled Ava, and he was probably trying to recreate his sister to make himself not feel guilty anymore.

Isaac wracked his brain for more places they had played at as children. Where else would he want to take his sister if she were alive?

Isaac shot up out of his chair.

Ian must have taken her to the place where his sister had died. There was an old shack they used to play in by the pond where Ava had drowned. Maybe he was stashing Olivia and Jill there.

He had to tell the police! He had to protect her at all costs. Decision made, he grabbed his gun, pulled on some boots, and bolted out the door. Isaac sprinted down the lane, dialed 911 and told them what he knew, then he hung up and ran into the woods.

He wasn't going to wait for the police to arrive and assemble a team to go in the woods. Isaac figured the average time for police response was twenty minutes, and it would take them even longer to trek through the woods. If Isaac left now, he could be at the shack in only a few minutes. It would be dangerous, but he couldn't just wait around and waste precious minutes.

A sense of urgency filled him. He just knew in his heart that he didn't have much time. If he didn't go now, he'd regret it for the rest of his life.

*

"Everything's going to be okay, Jill," Olivia whispered as Ian loaded some things into the car. "I know this is scary, but you are being really brave. I didn't want to bring him to the hospital to find you, but I didn't know what else to do. I'm trying to get you home, okay? I'll get you home, Jill. I promise. Don't worry."

Liv meant it. She would get Jill home, even if it was the last thing she would do. Jill nodded somberly, then Ian came back into the shack.

"Let's get in the car. I'll bring Ava first." Ian picked up a wriggling

Jill and carried her out the door.

Liv sighed heavily, her heart wrenching for the little girl. It was morning, and someone must have realized they were gone by now. Would Isaac remember Ian? Did he even know where Ava had drowned?

She just kept on praying Isaac would be able to lead the police here.

Ian came back inside and cut her ropes off and tied her hands together. He led her to the car.

"Oh, I forgot something," he muttered, then went back inside. "Wait here, Olivia."

"I'm scared," Jill cried from the back seat. Her brown eyes were wide with fear, and her small hands trembled.

"It will all be okay, I promise," Liv said.

She hoped it would be true.

Chapter Fourteen

Isaac raced through the woods, gun in hand. He sprinted toward the shack, branches whipping at his hands and face, but he didn't feel the pain. He had one goal in mind, and nothing else mattered.

He reached the pond and saw the shack. Behind it, hidden in the trees, was a car. Someone was there. Was it Ian? Where was he taking Liv and Jill?

Isaac crept toward the shack and hid behind a large bush. Now that he was closer, he heard voices.

"Oh, I forgot something. Wait here, Olivia," came a man's rumbling voice.

Olivia! She was alive. Where was Jill? Maybe she was still in the shack.

Footsteps crunched twigs. Isaac readied himself, heart pounding, gripping his Walther P99.

This was his one chance. His only shot.

He watched Ian go into the shack then waited for him to come back out. Isaac wanted to see his face first, just to make sure it was Ian. Waiting for him to come out was complete torture. Though it was only a few minutes, it seemed like an hour.

A door shut, and the man came out from behind the shack.

It was him. It was Ian!

Isaac aimed his gun at Ian's torso, the area of the body that was easiest to hit. He hoped he wouldn't kill him, but he had to injure him enough for Jill and Olivia to escape. He steadied his aim, then fired. The gunfire exploded in his ears along with Ian's screams as his face contorted and he crumpled to the ground. In the distance, Liv shouted something.

A dark, angry, endless crimson flowed from Ian's leg. The hours Isaac had spent target shooting with this new gun had paid off. At least he had missed the torso and only hit the leg.

Isaac waited for remorse to set in, for him to regret what he had just done. But all he felt was relief. Isaac stood, and once Ian saw him, Ian shouted at Isaac.

"How could you?" Ian demanded, grabbing his leg with both hands and letting out a string of profanities.

"How could you kidnap an innocent woman and a girl?" Isaac shot back. He didn't wait for an answer. Gun aimed at Ian, Isaac slowly approached the criminal. He patted Ian down, checking for any weapons. He didn't have any on him.

Finally, Liv and Jill were safe. He reached the car and opened the door, helping Liv out.

"Isaac!" she cried out, and he ran and embraced her. He pressed his face into her hair, breathing in her vanilla scent mixed with dirt and fear. He'd never let her go. Never, ever again.

"I prayed that you would come rescue us," she cried into his shoulder.

"Once I heard you were gone, I knew Ian had kidnapped you since Samuel is in custody. And then I remembered that Ava had drowned here. I called the police and ran straight here. I couldn't wait for them. I had a feeling there wasn't much time left. Looks like I was right."

"Thank you," Liv said softly, her bound hands reaching up to his face.

"What happened?" Jill asked. Isaac turned to see her tied up, sitting in the back seat.

"Isaac rescued us. Stay there, okay?"

Isaac pulled out the pocket knife he had bought along with his gun and cut off their ropes. He took one and threw it at Ian. "Tie this around your leg."

"I'll kill you for this! You hear me? I will make you pay for this!" Ian screamed, then tied the rope tightly around his leg above the gunshot wound to slow the bleeding.

"What do we do now?" Liv asked, ignoring Ian. "I guess we could put him in the trunk for now. We don't want him trying anything."

They took the ropes, tied up Ian and carefully placed him in the trunk as he continued to yell threats and curse words. Liv hurried back to the shack to get her cell phone and put the battery back in it. She also grabbed Ian's Glock. She called CPDU and let them know what was going on, and they agreed to meet at the edge of the woods.

"Do you think that's the gun he used to kill Bill Sullivan and Bishop Johnson?" Isaac asked when he saw the Glock. They got in the car and Liv drove toward the community.

She explained, "Ian already confessed. But we can actually use the casing I found at Bishop Johnson's house to see if this gun was used to fire it. Glocks have rectangular firing pins, and when the gun fires, the firing pin makes a rectangular indentation on the primer. That's the middle part of the bullet. If we look at the firing pin indent and it is rectangular, that will tell us it was most likely fired by a Glock. A microscopic examination will compare the gun and casing to see if that specific gun cased the scrapes on that specific casing. Basically, if we look at the gun and the casing, we will be able to tell if they are a match. But Ian already told me he shot Bill and Bishop Johnson."

"Wow. That is fascinating!" Isaac's eyes widened in wonder.

"We have a lot of equipment that helps us solve crimes."

"I'd really like to learn more about it."

"Well, I'd be happy to teach you." She meant it, but as soon as she said the words, guilt and dread tore through her. It was almost time for her to leave.

After they reached the community, soon several police officers crowded the fields along with an ambulance.

In a chaos of shouting, police officers helping them and the paramedics taking Ian, somehow Jill squeezed her way through the crowd once she saw her mother.

"*Mamm!*" she called, her lavender dress flapping behind her, her blonde hair streaming like ribbons on a bicycle. She leapt into Mrs. Johnson's arms, who began to weep.

Isaac watched the tender sight, and it warmed his heart. Isaac knew that was what Olivia lived and worked for—seeing victims being reunited with their families.

Diana came out of her house, and once she recognized Ian, she ran at him, shouting his name. The officers held her back as the paramedics treated him, but Diana only cried out louder, calling out toward her long lost son, realizing her second son was being arrested.

The police officers whisked Liv and Isaac away to be questioned.

The entire time he was being questioned, Isaac kept glancing at Liv. She'd been through so much, and he just wanted to make sure she was all right. Once the officers and paramedics were finished with him, his family surrounded him.

"Isaac!" they cried, all hugging him at once.

"We are so glad you are all okay." Tears streamed down Hannah's face.

"I heard the police say your son shot a man." Bishop Byler stepped into their conversation.

His entire family gasped. "Is this true?" Amos whispered.

"The man was a killer. He kidnapped Liv and Jill. What was I supposed to do, let him take them out of the state? If they had gone, who knows if we would have ever found them alive! Yes, I shot him. I didn't kill him, only injured him to stop him. I thought it was the right thing to do," Isaac explained.

"You had a gun?" Hannah cried. "For hunting, you mean?"

"No, not for hunting. I got a handgun to carry for protection after the rash of crimes broke out. I thought it was the right choice," Isaac answered. And he didn't regret his decision one bit.

"Isaac, I know many of us have firearms for hunting, but this one represents self-defense and violence toward another person. I will dismiss this incident under the circumstances, but now that the culprit is caught, it is time to get rid of the pistol because of what it represents for you. Understand?" Bishop Byler asked.

Isaac was glad this bishop was understanding, but he wasn't sure about what his answer would be.

"You'll get rid of the gun, won't you, son?" Amos asked, his eyes pleading.

"I don't know," he said plainly and walked away.

"Isaac!"

Isaac turned to see Officer Martin jogging up to him. "I hear you did a heck of a job out there today. Liv won't stop raving about you."

Isaac blushed and looked away. "I just wanted to protect her and Jill."

"Well, I hear you shot Ian's legs in the first shot. You shot him in a place where he will be able to recover, yet injured him enough for him to no longer be a threat. You could have shot him anywhere on his body, but you were so precise. And you didn't let your emotions get in the way of the goal. For someone with no official training, you were excellent. Ever thought of becoming a police officer?" Jefferson asked, his eyes twinkling in the sunlight.

Isaac laughed out loud. "Me, a police officer?"

"Yeah. I think you'd be a great officer. You should think about it," Jefferson clapped him on the shoulder. "You're a great shot, and from what I hear, you're always calm in a situation. You always do the right thing."

"You do realize I'd be shunned if I became an officer, right? As in, my family wouldn't be allowed to talk to me anymore?" Isaac asked gently.

"Well, I guess that's your call. Sometimes if you really want something, it is worth making huge sacrifices for."

Isaac's gaze wandered to Liv. Would he be willing to sacrifice everything to be with her?

"Anyway, I just wanted to tell you that you did a good job, and that Liv really cares about you." Isaac detected jealously in Jefferson's voice. "So I hope you make the right decision."

"Thanks, Officer Martin." Isaac patted him on the back. He saw Liv finish her questioning, and he walked over to her.

"You okay?" He reached out to touch her arm.

She let out a long breath. "Yeah. Now that we know he committed all those crimes, I'm glad to know he'll probably be going to jail for life. Except we still don't know who attacked you. I don't think it was him." She glanced at Ian, who was on a stretcher. The paramedics prepared him to be put in the ambulance. "My partner told me the test results of the bat did not match the wood splinters that were found in your head. The perp must have worn gloves. His prints weren't on it. None on the step, either. So that probably wasn't the weapon you were attacked with. He couldn't find any prints on the note that was left in your house, either, but Ian admitted to leaving it."

Isaac shrugged. "I guess not all mysteries can be solved."

"But I still want to investigate why the word *help* was on the Sullivans' window," she whispered, leaning toward him. "It might give us more answers."

"Well, just don't get your hopes up. We could end up with no answers, just like when your house was burned down."

211

*

Liv sucked in a breath, remembering what Ian had said in the shack when she had asked him if he had burned down Sid's barn.

I like fire…

This was her chance. She had to know if he was the one who killed her family.

Liv whipped around and ran towards Ian, who was about to be put into the ambulance.

"I want to ask him one question. It'll just take a second," she said to a paramedic, pushing her way through and flashing her badge. She marched up to Ian. "Did you burn down my house?"

Ian turned his head and stared at her, his cold eyes void of any compassion.

"Did you kill my family?" she demanded, even louder this time.

Ian chuckled. It was an irritating sound, like nails scraping a chalkboard.

"Come on, Ian, you're getting life in prison. Confessing to one more crime won't make much of a difference. You told me earlier you like fire. You were hinting that you were the arsonist who burned down my house, weren't you?"

Ian narrowed his icy blue eyes, staring her down. "Yes, I was. You're a smart girl, and I knew you'd figure it out."

"Why did you kill them?" Liv cried. Isaac ran up behind her and grabbed her arm, but she pushed him away.

"Your little sister was just like Ava. The same age, same height. Same hair color. What was her name again?" Ian smirked.

"Beth! You know her name was Beth!" Liv screamed. Tears stung her eyes. No, she would not cry in front of all these people, people she worked with. She held her tears back, balling her hands into fists.

"Your family was so perfect back then. I couldn't stand to see you all together, one big happy family, with a little girl just like Ava. I had to kill you all. What I didn't know was that you weren't in the house at the time, until I saw you running back after I had already set the fire." Ian's lip curled into a snarl. "And I couldn't bring myself to kill you then. I liked watching you, wishing you could save them. But you couldn't."

Liv recalled the memory of him standing in the shadows, wearing that hideous angry clown mask. She shivered, her skin crawling with disgust.

"You should have died that day with them. I should have killed you, too. Then my brother would still be alive, and none of this would have ever happened! It's all your fault!"

"No!" Liv screamed, grabbing onto the side of the stretcher for support. When Ian touched her hand, she yanked herself away and started to collapse, but Isaac caught her in his strong arms.

As the paramedics lifted the criminal up into the ambulance, Isaac led Liv to the edge of the field, away from everyone else. The crowd started to clear, and he knew she wanted to cry.

"He killed them all!" Her tears flowed freely now. She grabbed onto him and sobbed into his chest, her body wracking with each breath. "Maybe he should have killed me that day. He was right. Then none of this would have happened!" Her voice was muffled by his shirt.

Isaac pulled away enough to see her face, and he held her chin in his hand. "No. He's a liar and a sociopath. He only said that to hurt you. He still would have come here and killed his father, killed the bishop, and committed those crimes. None of this is your fault, Liv."

Never before had Isaac ever seen Liv cry. She had always been so strong, but after a horrific chain of events, this finally broke her. He held her in his arms until she stopped crying, under the shade of the trees, until her tears ran out.

*

Once Liv finally recovered, she called Captain Branson.

"The killer has been found. Why don't you want to come back to CPDU? You never even wanted to go to Amishland in the first place. Now you want to stay longer? It's getting boring here without you joking around and pranking people," Branson said.

"I just need a little more time. I need to figure out what is going on at the Sullivan's house," she explained. "After I saw the word *help* written on the basement window, I searched and didn't find anything, but I want to look for clues one more time. Plus, we never discovered who attacked Isaac. The bat wasn't a match on the weapon used to attack him."

"Well, just so you know, now that we know Ian is the perp, we released Samuel from custody. We didn't have enough to hold Samuel." She heard Branson slam shut the filing cabinet in his office and slap a stack of papers on his wooden desk.

"It's fine. I'll be careful. So may I stay a few days longer?"

"Yes, you may."

"Thank you, sir."

She hung up and sat back in her chair on the porch at the Mast farm, listening to the sounds of the animals. She looked across the farmland to the Sullivans' house. Now that Samuel was back, Liv would have to be extra careful about investigating what was going on in his house. If only she could go up to his front door and tell him she needed to search his house immediately. But that would completely blow her cover, and if she was wrong about Samuel, that could be a disaster.

"Why did you become a police officer?" Isaac asked Liv, looking at her as he sat next to her on the porch.

"I wanted to help people get the justice I never had. And to get answers I never had. I just wanted to help people get out of situations like I was in." She let out a slow breath, looking up at the cloudy sky.

"What was it like living with Jake?" he asked.

Liv brought her feet up onto the chair and clammed up. She had never told anyone what it had been like, not in detail.

"You don't have to answer that," Isaac murmured, looking embarrassed. "Sorry."

"You know what? It's okay. It's time I talk about it." She set her feet back down on the boards of the porch. She looked at Isaac. "Every day I lived in fear. My world was fear. It was how he controlled me. It was all I knew after a while."

Isaac shifted in his seat, turning to her so he could hold her hand.

She smiled a little at his touch, then continued. "I felt like my life was dark and hopeless. Like there was no way out, like it would be horrible forever. He blamed me for everything. Even if I had nothing to do with it, he'd find a way to blame me. He criticized everything about me. He critiqued how I stood, how I walked and talked. He told me I had an ugly laugh and that I couldn't walk straight. He always had something to complain about. He hated that I couldn't cook or sew well or be like any other 'good' Amish woman. To him, I was nothing. And he didn't hesitate to tell me that. He told me I wasn't good enough for him, and he told me he didn't even know why he married me. But he said he was stuck with me because there is no such thing as divorce in the eyes of the church."

Liv paused, taking in a deep breath, calming herself down when memories resurfaced like a dark whale coming up to the surface of the sea.

Isaac's eyes shone with tears, and one tear fell, trickling down his face. "That day I bumped into you in the grocery store, you spilled your groceries everywhere, and I saw that huge bruise on your arm. Remember?"

She nodded. She had known that day when he had seen her bruised arm that he suspected Jake was abusive even before that.

"What happened that day, the day he died? I saw the way Jake walked up to us and dug his fingers into your arm so inconspicuously so no one would notice, but I did. I saw the anger in his eyes. You told me a little about what happened, but not the full story."

She trembled at the memory of Isaac's face as Jake had walked her out of the store. Isaac had looked so worried. "He accused me of having an affair with you. Can you believe that? He asked me why I didn't look at him like that, but how could I shower him with love when I spent every second wondering when he was going to hit me next?"

"Oh, Liv. I don't even know what to say. That happened because I talked to you in the store, didn't it? Is it my fault?"

Liv stood up and walked to the porch railing. "No, of course not. He would have tried to kill me sooner or later. Don't you dare blame yourself." She looked at him, eyebrows drawn together. "Promise me."

He sighed, giving a weak smile, and got up to stand beside her. "I will try. But I can't stop thinking about how I should have convinced you to marry me instead. Then none of that would have happened. I would have protected you. And loved you more than life itself."

She thought for a moment he might kiss her, but she knew he wouldn't out here on her uncle's porch.

"Remember when I ran to your house, right after Jake died? You told me you should have married me then, too." She took in a shaky breath as the memories washed over her, how she had taken a fistful of his thick, dark hair and kissed him. He had told her he would have taken care of her, and that Jake hadn't deserved her. He held her bruised body in his arms, even though she was covered in blood.

It had felt so right, yet so wrong, and it had been terrible timing.

And then she had left him there because he refused to go with her.

"Yes, I did say that. I meant it then, too. Come on. Let's walk." Isaac reached out and gently took hold of her hand, and she couldn't pull away. She let him lead her down the porch steps, and they stepped out onto the grass.

"Everything happens for a reason, Isaac. You taught me that. If I had married you, I never would have become a police officer. Then I wouldn't have been able to help all the people I have helped. Jill might have been killed if I hadn't been here to investigate. And if you had not have helped. The truth is, being with Jake made me strong enough for this job. I'm not sure I could have ever been able to do it if I hadn't married him. Sad as that is."

"You're right. Everything does happen for a reason. But I still can't believe Ian was the arsonist who killed your family. What happened that night?" Isaac asked gently. When she didn't respond right away, he said, "You don't have to answer if you don't want to."

She looked at him again. "No, I'll tell you. That was the night I sneaked out to see you. I threw pebbles at your window, remember? We talked for a while as I stood outside your window, then I ran back home. When I got there, the house was overtaken by flames. I didn't know what to do. I wanted to rescue them, but I knew I couldn't. It was too late. Then I saw a shadow moving, and I saw Ian. He was wearing an angry clown mask. We looked at each other, then he walked away. He could have killed me, but he just watched me watch my house burn down. He took away everything I loved." One tear spilled over onto her cheek.

Isaac stopped walking, so Liv did too. They stood in front of the woods.

"But you got through it somehow." He stared at her a moment in awe. "You know, Liv, you are the strongest person I have ever met.

No matter what you face, you remain strong."

Liv smiled shyly, blushing. "Thanks, Isaac."

She could tell he meant it as she looked up into his green eyes, glowing with what she knew was love for her. She felt so unworthy of his love, but she knew he'd insist on the contrary.

The truth was, she loved him so much it hurt. She couldn't have ever lied about that. She reached up, touched his face, and smiled. Liv didn't think about leaving, or the case. Just Isaac, here and now in this moment together.

He covered her hand with his and whispered, "I love you."

Her heart twisted in agony because she couldn't stay. But she ignored that fact, too.

If all she had was right now, she'd regret it for the rest of her life if she didn't kiss him.

He stared at her, and for a moment she wondered if he could see inside her mind. She looked into those green eyes again, unable to look away even if she wanted to. She thought of every moment they had ever spent together, from their dating days as teens, to the day she had gone to him after killing Jake, and all of the time they had spent together since she had returned. No one had ever been there for her like Isaac had.

"Liv, please. Kiss me."

She grabbed his suspenders and brought her lips up to his. He wrapped his arms around her, then he pulled away after a moment, but she pulled him right back. Joy, excitement, and longing filled her. The world slipped away, and all that was left was the two of them. Nothing else mattered. She reached up and grabbed a fistful of his wavy hair and took in a deep breath, finally leaning back to look at his face.

"I'm sorry about that," he stammered, turning red. "We aren't supposed to kiss until marriage."

"Oh... Right." Embarrassment colored her cheeks. What had she been thinking? Kissing Isaac was not part of the job description.

"Look, I'd love to kiss you again, but we can't. Not just because it is against the *Ordnung*. I personally believe that the body is a temple of the Holy Spirit, as it says in the Bible, and that we are to keep ourselves completely pure until marriage. Okay? That means no kissing."

She sighed. She had grown up on the same principles. Besides, she really shouldn't be kissing him when she would only have to leave soon. She would only become more attached to him, making it harder for the both of them when she left.

Who was she kidding? Liv was already very attached to him.

"You're totally right, Isaac. I'm sorry, too."

"It's okay. We just have to be more careful."

"Listen," he said as they continued to walk. "I haven't really been able to talk to you much about your faith. I know you are considering staying here, but what about your faith? If you did leave, would you at least remain Christian?"

Guilt stabbed through Liv when she remembered she had lied to Isaac when she told him she was considering staying. She had had to in order to get him to help her.

"Well, if I did leave I would definitely still want to be Christian," she said, telling the truth. "I miss the close relationship I used to have with God. But I'm not sure if I can ever get that back."

"Sure you can."

"Isaac, I've killed people," she blurted. "I had to shoot kidnappers and murderers while doing my job, but it was always in protection of myself or others. I know God says not to murder, and I don't think that is considered murder if they were threatening lives, but do you think He thinks it is?"

"I don't think so. But either way, God will forgive you if you ask Him." Isaac squeezed her hand.

Liv had expected Isaac to shrink back at her confession, but he remained by her side. Nothing seemed to fluster him.

"Well, I have done a good job of ignoring Him all these years," she muttered.

"Come on, Liv. You know God still loves you and wants you back. You've just got to repent and start reading your Bible and praying again. That's how you'll get close to Him." Isaac gave her a gentle smile, his thumb drawing circles on her hand.

"I know," she sighed. "But sometimes I feel awkward praying or reading the Bible. Like I'm unworthy."

"Well, you're right. We are unworthy of God's love. But don't feel awkward talking to Him. He loves you more than you will ever know. It might only be awkward at first."

"You're right, Isaac. You're absolutely right." She looked out into the fields again. "I'm going to start reading my Bible and praying again."

As they continued walking, they approached the Sullivan's house. Liv peered closer.

"Look, Isaac!"

The word *help* was written on the basement window again.

"I have to go in there. Someone inside needs help." Liv bolted toward the house, Isaac following close behind.

Chapter Fifteen

Liv ran to the Sullivan's driveway and their barn as Isaac continued to follow her.

"Diana and Samuel aren't home. Their buggy is gone." Liv ran around the back and opened the door. It was unlocked, of course. "You should stay here."

"What? No. I can help you. I'm coming with you. And don't you need a search warrant or something?" Isaac asked.

"Not if someone is in imminent danger. It's called exigent circumstances. That writing on the window tells me someone needs immediate help." Liv walked inside, opened the basement door and went down the stairs.

"Okay, now let's look for some type of lever or secret door. Sometimes it can be hidden behind something like furniture. One time I found one underneath a washing machine," Liv whispered, starting to feel along the cement walls for cracks.

Isaac nodded then started searching. For several minutes they felt along every wall, looked behind every box or piece of furniture.

Liv sighed. "Maybe I was wrong."

"No, don't give up yet. We're already here. Let's keep looking. He might have hidden it really well." He approached the wood pile and looked behind the stacks of wood, his hands grazing over the roughness of the wood.

Something in his mind twitched, a flash of a memory appearing for a moment. The feeling of the rough, splintery wood in his hands came back to him as he had stacked it here.

With Samuel's voice in the background.

Instantly Isaac knew he had been here recently. He reached up to his head and felt the bump that was still there. Is this the place where he had been injured?

Simultaneously, like water flowing from several streams into the ocean, the memories of his attack came rushing in.

He had been talking and laughing with Samuel, helping him stack the wood. Isaac dropped a piece and bent over, retrieving it. That was when the lever had been pushed down by the wood, lever that blended in so well with the stacks of firewood. Then sharp pain had rattled the back of his skull and knocked him to the floor.

Samuel had knocked him out with a piece of firewood.

"Liv!" he whispered, calling her over. He told her about his memories.

"That was why they found traces of wood in your head!" She kept her voice low. "Do you remember where the lever is?"

Isaac felt around, poking around with his flashlight.

There it was.

A concealed wooden lever which could easily be mistaken for a piece of firewood in the stack.

They looked at each other, then Isaac pushed it down. The rectangle shape of a door appeared, something they never would have noticed before. A secret door, hiding who knows what—or who.

Liv stepped forward gingerly, seeing a light on in the secret room which instantly was turned off. She raised her gun and swept the room.

"Police! Who is in there?"

There was no answer, but there was a shuffling noise. There was a small bed, a toilet, a dresser, and a desk in the corner.

A thin, pale young woman cowered there, shaking in fear.

A thousand questions clamored in Liv's mind. She had been right. But why was this woman locked in here? "What is your name?"

"You saw what I wrote on the window?"

"Yes. That's why we're here. To get you out."

"I thought I wanted to escape, but I'm too afraid. You should go," the woman said, hiding behind the dresser in the corner. "Please. Just go. And don't tell anyone I'm here."

"No. I can't do that. My name is Olivia Mast, and I'm an undercover police detective. This is Isaac Troyer. He lives in this community. Now, I need to know your name."

The woman only stared at her, trembling.

"Please, will you tell me your name?" Liv said.

"My name..." The woman spoke barely above a whisper. "My name is Ava Sullivan."

"Ava?" Isaac and Liv both whispered in unison.

"Everyone thinks you're dead," Liv told her, shaking her head. There was so much to tell this woman, and so much to ask her, but they only had a few minutes. "Why are you down here?"

"Really, you can't be here. If Samuel finds out, it will be very bad," she stammered, pushing her blonde hair out of her brown eyes. "My mother and brother went out to run errands, but they could be back any minute."

Ava did look a little like an older version of Jill Johnson. A thin, pale, timid older version. She also resembled Liv's deceased little sister, Beth.

Liv pushed those thoughts from her mind. "Look, I won't let Samuel hurt you ever again. Please, just tell us why you are down here. So you wrote *help* on the window today and the other day?"

"Yes. Sometimes they let me out into that room for a little while. Sometimes I write *help* on the window, but no one has ever seen it or done anything about it...until now. I did it the other day too, but then I got afraid Samuel would see it so I wiped it off after a little bit."

"I saw it. That's the reason why we came. Who kept you down here? Was it your parents and Samuel?" Liv asked.

Ava nodded slowly. "My father put me down here when I was little. My mother always knew, and Samuel has known since my father died."

Liv went into the other room and quickly used her cell phone to call her captain. He agreed to send backup to arrest Diana and Samuel.

"Look, I know we have so much more to talk about. But it's not safe for us to stay here. We need to get you out now, okay?" Liv reached out her hand. As she walked closer to Ava, she noticed neat stacks of paper covered in writing. One of the top pages said *Freedom: a novel by Ava Sullivan*. Another stack had a paper on top of that one that read *The Secret City: a novel by Ava Sullivan.* There were a few more stacks that Liv guessed were manuscripts as well.

Well. Ava certainly had been busy during her time down here.

Ava darted back to the corner like a threatened mouse. "No! Samuel will find out! He'll be so angry! He'll hurt me, and probably you too."

"I told you, we won't let him hurt you."

"No. I can't go with you!"

A door upstairs opened. *Boom boom boom.* Samuel's footsteps pounded upstairs, resonating through the basement.

"They are home!" Ava whispered.

"Come on. We have to go right now. You'll be safe with us." Isaac stepped sideways to get closer to her. He bumped into a table with a metal bin on top of it which promptly fell on the concrete floor with a crashing bang.

Liv winced. "What, are you trying to wake up the dead? Let's go. Now."

"He heard us. Come on, Ava," Liv beckoned for Ava to come.

"I can't!" she cried, keeping a hand on the cold wall.

"This may be your only chance of escape!" Isaac backed out of the room.

Liv ran to the side of the stairs, planning to knock Samuel out once he ran by her.

"Get her out of here!" Liv told Isaac.

"She won't come!" Isaac cried, trying to coax Ava out of the room.

"Throw her over your shoulder, drag her, carry her, I don't care. Just get her out!"

The cellar door flung open, and Samuel bounded down the steps. "Who is down there?" he yelled. Once Samuel was past her, Liv lunged at him, trying to knock him out with the edge of her .45, but he darted away and she missed. He threw a punch at her, and she dodged it, spinning around into a roundhouse kick, her foot hitting his side.

He stumbled, then saw Isaac. Samuel turned and jumped on top of Isaac, tackling him to the floor.

"I told you to stay away from here!" Samuel shouted, punching Isaac in the face.

"No!" Liv screamed, trying to kick Samuel off Isaac. Isaac fought Samuel back, but he was no match for the angry criminal.

Liv pushed Samuel, and he lost his balance. Liv brought the gun down on his head as hard as she could, knocking him out. He crumpled to the floor, and Liv pulled out one of two pairs of handcuffs that she had attached to her holster and handcuffed him.

"The police should be here any second," Liv said, seeing Ava standing in the doorway. "I called them."

"What about *Mamm*?" Ava asked.

As if on cue, Diana ran down the steps. "Samuel? Samuel!"

Diana looked at Samuel slumped against the wall, Ava standing in the doorway, Isaac watching, and then Diana's eyes fell on Liv and her gun.

"What did you do?" she screamed, raging towards Liv. Diana struck out at her, but Liv blocked it, firmly grabbing Diana's arms and pulling them behind her back, snapping another pair of handcuffs onto them.

Liv said, "Diana Sullivan, you are under arrest. Anything you say can and will be used against you in a court of law—"

"No! You can't do this. I was protecting her!" Diana shouted, trying to wriggle free, but Isaac came and helped Liv hold her still.

Liv finished reciting her Miranda rights. "Diana, I am a detective from Covert Police Detectives Unit. And yes, I can do this. What you didn't have the right to do was hold your daughter captive here for almost her entire life."

Diana's eyes darted back and forth between the only two children she had left. Liv watched as Diana realized she and Samuel would go to prison and Ava would be set free.

Diana whipped her head around to face Liv and cried out, "You took all my children away from me!" She let out a scream of frustration, then collapsed to the floor.

Liv knelt down next to Diana and whispered, "I know you were a victim of the abuse from your husband as I was a victim of Jake's abuse, even though you denied it. You went through the same thing I did. You and I have a lot in common. But I would never, ever hurt someone else on purpose like you hurt Ava. I was defending my own life when Jake died. You stole years from Ava when you could have set her free, and there is no excuse for that."

"But we would have gone to prison!"

"And now you are." Liv stood up and looked out the window to see flashing red and blue lights from the police officers responding to her call for backup. Officers stormed into the building and led Samuel and Diana away.

Ava watched as the commotion died down, silently standing in the doorway. Liv and Isaac stood by her.

"Ready to go?" Liv held out her hand to Ava. Who knew what she had been through these past two decades of her life?

Ava's soft brown eyes fell on Liv's outstretched hand offering freedom. Would Ava be brave enough to take it?

Liv grinned, feeling an overflowing joy as Ava took her hand. She led her outside, Isaac close behind.

As they stepped out of the house and onto the grass, Ava shielded her eyes from the setting sun. She probably hadn't seen sunlight in so long.

"You're very brave, Ava."

Ava just looked around wildly at all of the fields, trees, and farms, taking it all in. Liv couldn't imagine how she must be feeling. Happy? Excited? Afraid? Overwhelmed?

Several families had heard the police sirens and were crowding around outside to see what all the ruckus was about. When they saw Liv walking Ava out of the house, people gasped.

"That's Ava Sullivan!" a woman shouted, recognizing her. "She's alive!"

More people gathered around, all asking questions and talking amongst themselves. Liv, Isaac, and Ava watched as Samuel and Diana were taken away in police cars.

"I can't believe this is finally all over," Ava said quietly.

"Ava, you may have to testify in court about this."

Ava gave her a timid look. "Testify? Oh, no, I couldn't possibly."

"You're a lot stronger than you think. I can tell," Liv told her. "So, why did they keep you down there all those years? What happened?"

"Well, it all started the day my father tried to kill my mother. I saw him try to choke her. I walked in on it. I was maybe five or six, and they were afraid I would tell someone. So my father came up with a plan. He brought us kids to the pond to swim, then left us there, telling Ian he was in charge of watching me because he was the oldest. Then, while my brothers were playing a game with their friends and not paying attention, my father came back and snatched me away, telling me he'd hurt me if I made a noise. So I let him hide me away." Ava sighed and looked at the ground. "I couldn't fight him."

"Of course you couldn't. You were so young. It's not your fault." Liv wanted to reach out and pat her shoulder, but she was afraid Ava would shy away.

Ava continued, "He built that secret room himself, telling us never to go downstairs while he was working on it. He hid me that day he told everyone I drowned. He told me he was protecting me from the world. I think he meant he was protecting me from his own abuse. He beat my entire family. I think I might have been his favorite, and that's why he didn't want to hurt me anymore. I'm really not sure.

"He kept me down there so I wouldn't tell anyone about him trying to kill my mother, and I've been kept there ever since. My mother always knew, and she told Samuel about me after my father died."

"Your mother never tried to get you out?" Isaac asked.

"No. I think she was too afraid of what my father would do. But she loves me. She brought me books, paper, pencils, and art supplies. She tried to make the best of a terrible situation. Because of her, I was able to write all those novels you saw in there."

"That was kind of her." Liv wanted to add that Diana should have tried harder to get Ava out or at least tell the police, but now was not the time.

Ava nodded. "Yes. My father blamed Ian for supposedly letting me die. I don't know why. Maybe it was because he was the oldest child. It was one of his sick schemes. Ian left the Amish as soon as he was old enough. Haven't heard anything about him since then. My other brother Jake was killed by his wife several years ago, since he probably abused her too."

Liv winced, knowing Ava had no idea Liv was the one who had killed her brother.

"After I heard my father was murdered, Samuel and *Mamm* still wouldn't let me out. I guess they knew they would get in trouble if the secret got out." Ava took in a deep breath.

Isaac and Liv looked at each other, not knowing what to say.

After they took a moment to let her story sink in, Liv said, "Ava, I don't know what else to say except I'm so sorry you had to go through all that."

Ava looked up at the sky and stared at it as though she had never seen it before, then she looked at Liv. "Thank you for getting me out of there."

"I'm just glad you're safe now. So, what will you do with your freedom? I'm guessing you'll get to keep that house all to yourself while they are in prison. They will be in jail for a very, very long time."

Ava let out a sigh of relief. "You mean will I remain Amish? I am not really sure. Technically, I am Amish, but I never really got to live the lifestyle. I guess I am stuck between your world and mine," she sighed. "Maybe I should try both and then choose."

"That's a good idea. I was raised here, but I tried both worlds. Then I chose." A tightening feeling constricted her when she was reminded of what pain her choice would soon bring.

She would lose Isaac again.

"What did you choose? The *Englisher* life?"

"Yes. So I can keep on helping people like you," Liv told her, giving a small smile.

"Seems like a good enough reason to me. I think I want to help people too. I'd like to be an author or counselor. I've read a lot of college-level books that my mother brought to me in secret. But I'd have to give up the Amish life to go to school and do that as a career."

"My partner says sometimes doing something you really love is worth the sacrifices you have to make," Liv said as they reached the officers. They took Ava away for questioning, leaving Liv and Isaac standing there in the moonlight.

"Are you going to leave now that the case is solved?" Isaac's voice wavered.

Liv started walking with him toward the trees, away from all the bystanders and officers. "Isaac, you know I wouldn't last a month here."

He let out a breath of frustration. "I was hoping you'd fall in love with this place."

"I have. I do love it here. I love all the people here. I just don't belong here. I need to be out there, helping people, or else I'll go insane. The Amish people are great and so unified, but the rules are just too constricting for me. I'm sorry, Isaac. Have you thought more about coming to live in the *Englisher* world?"

"Yes. But I'd hate to leave my family and my home and everything I know. I don't think I'd ever fit in your world. Isn't there some way we can work something out so we are both happy?" Isaac persisted, grasping for some hope.

"The only way this will end is with both of us miserable."

"But don't you love me?" Isaac asked. "You really don't think you could live here to be with me?"

Liv paused. If she left him behind knowing she loved him, he'd never move on. She had to face the truth—this would never work. Either one of them would be miserable or both. She couldn't expect him to leave everything he loved behind just to be with her. He would be shunned, unable to talk to his family if he left. And her living here was just not an option.

"Isaac, I lied to you. The truth is, I just never loved you these past several days. This was all a part of my cover. I needed you to help me with the investigation, so I had to lead you on. I'm sorry." She forced the words out in one fast, agonizing breath.

The truth was that she loved him so much she'd do anything for him, anything to protect him, even if that meant lying to him. She had to make this choice for him or else she knew he would spend his entire life asking himself *what if?*

"Come on, Liv. Are you serious?" He smiled at first, then it dropped off his face when he saw her grave expression. "Oh. You really are serious, aren't you? You don't…you don't love me at all?"

"No. I'm sorry. I really don't love you at all. Sorry I had to use you," she stated emotionlessly, flatly, while sorrow and grief tore her apart inside. She masked her anguish with an indifferent face. Just by looking at him, she knew he was having a hard time even standing up. "If you must know, I am engaged to Officer Martin."

"What? He didn't mention that." He grabbed the sides of his head as if he was about to rip his hair out. "You lied to me this entire time? Every look, the kiss, all the things we talked about? Do you even want to remain a Christian? Or was that phony too?" he demanded, tears falling onto his red cheeks, green eyes shimmering with sadness and a thousand unasked questions.

"Yes. It was all a lie. Thank you for all your help. I'm sorry, Mr. Troyer." She used his last name for effect and walked away. Every step she took ripped an even bigger hole in her heart, scraping off little pieces of her soul. Sorrow weighed down on her like she was being crushed under a horse and buggy, almost crippling her.

I hope he finds happiness…and love. He deserves it.

She heard him begin to cry behind her, and she let her own tears fall.

But he would never know that she cried even one tear.

*

Liv didn't sleep for a second during the rest of the night at the Mast farm. Finally, the sun crept up over the hill, but Liv covered her red eyes. She had sobbed the entire night, shaking and reliving the conversation she had had with Isaac.

She must have devastated him. Crushed him. But it had been necessary.

"I really don't love you at all..."

A new wave of sobs came over her. She just couldn't stop crying. But she would have to get over this sooner or later and get back to her job. Her time with him here had been a fantasy, unrealistic. Maybe the stress of her job had messed with her head, ruining her judgment. It was beyond clear that there was no future for them, and now all she wanted for him was to move on and forget about her. And he would, with time, and he would realize it had just been an infatuation.

Knowing it was time to face Aunt Mary, Uncle Gideon and Maria, anxiety added to her sorrow. She packed up her few things and carried her bag downstairs. After her relatives said goodbye to her and she left, she would be shunned and they would no longer be allowed to speak to her or else they would be shunned themselves. The bishop and elders had graciously granted them one final goodbye as a thank you to Liv for stopping the killer.

Aunt Mary turned from the stove to face her, and Maria stopped setting the table. Uncle Gideon came into the kitchen. They all looked at her, not saying a word, looking terribly awkward.

"I'm so sorry... I wish I could have told you. I hope you understand I wasn't allowed to tell anyone," she blurted.

Maria and Aunt Mary rushed to her, Uncle Gideon following.

"We know, Olivia. We are just—" Aunt Mary choked up with tears, and her voice cracked. "We're so sad to see you go after thinking you had come back for good. Won't you please reconsider staying and repenting before the church?"

"I couldn't possibly stay. I belong out there. I love my job. I can't be Amish again. It's just not for me."

Once again Liv thought of Miranda, the last person she had helped by doing her job before returning to the community. She remembered the hope she had seen in her eyes, the way it felt to put away the horrible man who had kidnapped the child.

She knew her purpose in life was to lock up people like that and make Maine a safer place, little by little.

Maria wrapped her arms around her cousin and whispered into her ear, "We will miss you so much."

Liv teared up herself and swatted the tears away. "Stop it. You're going to make me cry." Then she heard a sniff behind her and turned to see Uncle Gideon with tears streaming down his face.

"Oh, Liv…"

She ran into his open arms. He held her for several minutes. "If you ever want to come back and truthfully become Amish again, you know you are welcome. If you ever decide to just ask the church for forgiveness and rejoin the faith, you know you would no longer be shunned."

Liv wiped her tears. "I know, but I really can't. I need to go back to my life and career. I don't deserve you guys. You've done so much for me, and all I did was lie to you. I don't even know how to thank you."

"You caught the criminals plaguing our community. That's more than enough of a thank you," Maria said, and her aunt and uncle nodded.

"We are proud of you, Liv," Aunt Mary said, holding Liv's face. "You were so brave to leave and follow your dreams. You are so good at your job, and you help so many people. That's more than any of us can do."

"You all do amazing things, too." Liv blushed. "There's no way I could have lived the life of hard work that you do. I mean, you have your own business and your own gardens and you build barns in one day."

"All work is good when done for the Lord," Uncle Gideon told her. "And you will stay Christian, we hope?"

"Yes, of course. I actually want to get much closer to God. I ignored Him for a long time, but that is over now."

"Good. That is all that really matters. Now, come sit and eat breakfast before it gets cold." Aunt Mary wiped her hands on her apron.

They gathered at the table and Uncle Gideon prayed, but Liv only picked at her oatmeal and eggs. Her thoughts kept returning to Isaac. Had he slept last night? Could he eat?

"What is it, Liv?" Aunt Mary asked, reaching for her hand.

"I'm so sad about Isaac. It would never have worked, but still." Liv wiped away another tear, her throat tightening at the mention of his name.

Uncle Gideon grabbed her other hand and gently squeezed it, and his rough and cracked skin from years of hard work felt more comforting than any fine silk or cashmere. "If you are meant to be together, it will happen. Maybe God has a plan for you two if you truly love each other."

"Sometimes true love isn't enough to make a relationship work." Liv sighed. Uncle Gideon rubbed her hand gently.

"But true love conquers all," Maria said wistfully, a hopeless romantic.

Maria lived a sheltered life compared to the evil, horrific things Liv saw consistently, but she didn't say so. She looked at Maria. "Not always. We'd need a miracle for Isaac and me to end up together."

*

"Isaac? Isaac!"

Isaac picked up his head after just resting his eyes for a moment.

"What are you doing? This order for the Millers is due tomorrow. We have to pick up the pace if we want to deliver it on time. Every time I look over at you, you look half asleep." Gideon inspected Isaac's half-sanded set of cabinets. Then his face softened. "You do look really tired."

"Well, I don't sleep much anymore." Isaac began to sand the wood again. His heart felt as heavy as these cabinets. He hadn't slept much at all since Liv left. How could she have lied to him that whole time? How could he have been so blind?

Even after how she had hurt him and lied to him, he still missed her. Still loved her, even though she didn't love him. That was the worst part.

Anna had wasted no time in trying to win Isaac back, but every time she tried talking to him, all he could think about was Liv. He wondered if he would ever get over her.

After she left, he had repented before the church about buying and using the pistol. He had not been shunned, but he felt as though he had been in a little bubble of isolation ever since Liv had left. Depression had begun to slink into his life, and he found himself avoiding people and being more withdrawn.

"Look, even though it has been two months since Olivia left, we all still miss her. But it's time to move on." Gideon lowered his voice. "You both told me you each knew it wouldn't work out."

"I know. I just keep thinking about her." Isaac dropped his hands.

"We all think about her. Just try not to let it affect your work. Okay?" Gideon gave him a concerned glance.

"You're right," Isaac said, focusing back on his job.

Gideon nodded and left him alone. A few minutes later, exhaustion took over Isaac. His eyes began to close. All he wanted to do was sleep, but every time he tried, all he saw was Liv's face. If he could close his eyes just for a minute he'd be fine.

"Isaac!"

Isaac snapped back to attention. He had fallen into a deep sleep, slumped over his work station.

"I'm so sorry, Gideon. I'm really not myself." He felt his face heat in embarrassment and shook his head at himself.

Gideon took the sander from him gently. "You should go home and get some rest so you can come in ready to go tomorrow. I'll have the guys finish this up. Okay?"

Isaac sighed. "Thank you. See you tomorrow." He picked himself up, grabbed his lunch bag and headed out the door.

The whole walk home he chided himself for how irresponsible he had been. He hadn't been the same since Liv had left. He had overslept twice, since he barely slept at night, and had been nodding off at work. He had mixed up an order, and one time he even wore a shirt inside out. It was as if Liv had not only stolen his heart but his brain as well.

Off in the distance, he saw Maria walking home with a few bags of groceries. It would be out of his way for him to help her carry them home, but he didn't mind at all.

"Hey, Maria!" he called, waving.

"Hi!" she said, staggering under the weight of the grocery bags. She walked up to him and looked at him more closely. "Wow, Isaac. You look awful." Suddenly she blushed. "I'm sorry, that came out wrong."

He held up a hand. "No, you're right. Your dad said the same thing, basically." He took more than half the bags from her. "Let me help you carry these home."

"You sure?"

"Definitely." He began walking with her towards the Mast farm. For a moment it was an awkward silence, then he asked the question they were both thinking.

"Heard from Liv?" he asked softly.

"Yeah. She wrote us a letter. I wish we could speak to her, but she's doing well." She gave him a sidelong glance. "She hasn't written to you or anything?"

"No. I wouldn't be surprised if she never spoke to me again, after the way she lied to me that whole time."

"She lied to all of us. She had to for her job," Maria said plainly as a bird flew over their heads.

"No, she lied to me the most, making me think she loved me when it was all for her cover. I mean, I understand why she had to—"

"Wait, what?" Maria shouted, dropping all her bags on the ground with a *thud.*

Isaac stopped and looked at the bags crumpled on the grass, frowning. "I hope there weren't eggs in those bags."

"Isaac! She must have lied to you!" Maria cried, grabbing his sleeves.

"I know. I just said that."

"No! No. She lied to you when she told you she doesn't love you."

"What?" A small glimmer of hope inside him lit like a burning ember.

"The morning she left, she was miserable! She knew it wouldn't work between you and her, but it was obvious that she is in love with you," Maria told him, shaking him. "And trust me, I know my own cousin. She probably told you she didn't love you so you'd forget about her and move on with your life. She said it would take a miracle for you two to end up together."

"Wait. She told me she is engaged to Officer Martin."

"No!" Maria laughed, stomping her foot. "She is such a little lying badger! I know she did this because she thought it was the right thing to do. Because she *loves* you!"

Isaac dropped his own bags and his hands flew up to his face. Could this be true? Did Liv really love him after all? Joy coursed through him like electricity, and for the first time in two months he felt happy. Hope filled him like air filled a newborn's lungs for the first time, bringing him to life.

"You have to talk to her," Maria told him. "Give me those bags. We're almost at my house anyway." She yanked the groceries back from him.

"You sure?"

"*Ja*! Just go!" she shouted, waving him away, smiling.

"I've got to go back to work and tell Gideon! I'll use the shop phone to call her," he blurted then ran back to the cabinet shop.

Chapter Sixteen

Olivia knocked on the door of a suspect's house. "Mr. Peters? Police. We just want to talk." No answer.

Jefferson gave her a questioning look.

She shrugged and knocked again, harder, almost pounding. "Come on, Peters, we know you're in there. We just want to ask you a few more—"

Gunfire rained down from an upstairs window, hitting a pot next to them, shattering it. As shards of pottery flew, Liv and Jefferson leapt off the porch and sprinted behind a shed for cover.

The shooter shouted profanities at them from the window, demanding that they leave.

"Wow!" Jefferson exclaimed, catching his breath. "He's got to have Bella Reeves in there. Why else would he shoot at us if he didn't kidnap her? He doesn't want us to find her. Or he really just doesn't like people on his property."

"Sounds about right to me." Liv peeked around the corner. Peters was still there, looking around for them. "Or he's crazy."

"What should we do?" Jefferson asked, and while Liv thought of a plan, he called CPDU for backup.

"They'll be here in ten minutes. But he might kill her in that time. We've got to get in there somehow." Liv bit her lip. "I saw a cellar door when we drove up. How about if you just talk to him while I sneak in the back door?"

"In case you forgot, he just shot at us!" Jefferson said, exasperated.

"I meant you can just stay here and talk to him from behind the shed. It's not that far. He'll be able to hear you, and he might not even notice I'm gone. Just keep him distracted so I can get in and look for Bella. Okay?" Liv looked around the corner and gripped her gun tightly.

"Okay. I guess so. But what if the door is locked? Let's go see. It probably is."

"Well, yeah. If I was hiding a kidnapped girl in my house, I'd keep all my doors locked, too," Liv remarked sarcastically as they darted across the lawn to the backyard. Peters hadn't been standing in the window, which really worried Liv.

She yanked on the cellar door, but it was locked tight. "I don't think I can pick this lock. Go make him mad so he starts shooting again, and I'll fire. Hopefully, he won't hear it over the noise."

"You want him to shoot at me?" Jefferson asked incredulously.

"No! Not *at* you. Just get him to shoot, okay?"

Jefferson darted around the side of the house and out of sight.

Liv aimed her pistol and waited. Jefferson yelled something snarky at Peters, then several shots were fired. Liv immediately shot at the door, busting it open. So far, so good. She yanked on the door again, and it gave way. She crept inside.

Liv turned on her flashlight and searched the room. She held up her M&P Shield as she poked her head around the corner.

She spent the next few minutes looking for some clue to where they could find Bella Reeves. Evidence suggested the kidnapper might be keeping her here. Olivia's heart pounded with the hope and anticipation of rescuing the girl. Hopefully, she was still alive. If she was, surely she was terrified. Olivia imagined her trembling in fear, and it spurred her on.

A soft whimper sounded in the darkness. *Oh, thank goodness.* The girl was alive. Bella was safe now. Liv aimed the beam of the flashlight at the corner of the room, and there was a teenaged girl with her hands tied and her mouth covered with duct tape, trembling in the glow of the flashlight. Bella looked terrified, her already big eyes widened with fear, her dark hair a tangled mess, dirt smudged on her face.

Olivia used to wonder if the anger would subside after doing this job for a few years. But the anger always came when she saw a victim of kidnapping—anger towards the kidnapper. Why did criminals think they had the right to do this to someone, especially a child?

"Bella, my name is Olivia, and I'm a police detective from a unit called CPDU. Can I come closer?"

The girl nodded. Olivia walked towards her slowly. "I'm going to take those ropes and the tape off." Bella nodded, and Liv pulled off the tape, then the ropes.

The girl whispered, "Where is he? Does he know you're here?"

Liv held still and listened closely, looking for any sign of movement among the stacks of dusty boxes and old furniture. She pushed her way through the cobwebs and clutter, sweeping her flashlight back and forth, Bella close beside her.

"My partner, Officer Martin, is outside distracting Peters. Now, I need you to listen closely. Right now I don't know where he is. He's probably upstairs, but he could be sneaking around outside. Backup is coming in a few minutes, and we need to get you out of here. So let's carefully make our way out that door, okay? Stay behind me."

The girl nodded, and Liv led her close to the door. The floor was so cluttered it was hard not to trip on anything.

Bella was going too fast, too hasty. Liv was about to tell her to slow down, but Bella tripped on a curtain rod that was lying across the floor, sending several heavy boxes toppling to the ground.

"Get out, now!" Liv ordered, aiming her gun at the stairs that led to the second floor. Bella ran for the door, and Liv backed out behind her. The kidnapper's loud footsteps pounded down the stairs, but she couldn't let the man out of this house without endangering Bella's life. Liv had to shoot at him now.

She waited for him to appear at the bottom of the steps.

"Police! Freeze or I'll shoot!" she hollered.

When he ignored her, she shot at him and hit him in the side, but he only clutched the wound, staggering briefly before continuing to lumber toward her. Hair flying and eyes raging, he looked manic with anger. A split-second glance told him Bella was gone. Liv shot his shoulder, and even though he was hit, he still lunged for her. She darted out of the way, but she tripped on something and crashed to the floor. She tried to get up and run, but he was too fast.

His eyes burned with an angry fire as he took a swing at her and pinned her against the washing machine. He wrapped his hands around her neck, squeezing harder and harder as he lifted her feet off the floor.

Not again…

Memories of Ian attacking her flashed through her mind. The way he had overpowered her, the way he had held a gun to her head. All the times Jake had abused her. But one memory overshadowed all others. Jake had tried to choke her just like this all those years ago, squeezing the life from her as she began to be overtaken by darkness. Back then in their simple kitchen, she had figured for a moment maybe it would be better if she was dead. She had let her eyes close, knowing she would go to a better place than the hell she had lived in.

That was when she had fought Jake for her life.

Her eyes opened.

She would fight back. Again.

She tried to punch him, but it was as if he didn't feel a thing. She tried to scream Jefferson's name, but her vocal chords were being crushed.

Peters grappled the firearm out of Liv's hand, nearly breaking her wrist. She cried out in pain, but he held her arms down as he pressed her against himself. She smelled his sweat and blood and cringed at the feeling of his skin. Peters then held her own gun to her head.

"Call your partner and tell him to send Bella back in here now. Alone." His fetid breath was hot in her ear. He groaned in pain.

When she hesitated, he yanked on her communicating device and shouted, "Do it now!"

Trembling, she took it and said into it, "Jefferson, send Bella back in here alone."

"What? I can't do that."

"And tell him if he doesn't do it within one minute, I'll kill you,"

Peters spat, clutching her even harder like a menacing grizzly bear grasping a wriggling fish in its claws.

"And Peters says if you don't do it in one minute, he'll kill me."

Was this how she would die? In the grasp of an insane kidnapper?

No. Liv trusted Jefferson to make the right decision. He was smart. She knew he'd come in here and somehow get her out of this situation. Somehow.

But Liv knew even if Jefferson did come down here and shoot, she'd be hit anyway because Peters was using her as a body shield. And if Jefferson came down here at all without Bella, Peters would kill Liv anyway.

Maybe this really was how she would die. Unless backup got here really soon, she was a dead woman.

The steps creaked. Someone was coming down to the cellar.

Jefferson.

Liv braced herself to fight. She waited...

Then Jefferson leapt into the room, shooting at the wall behind them. While Peters was distracted, Liv slammed her foot down on his leg sharply, bringing him down just long enough for her to elbow him in the nose and wiggle out of his arms. She bolted for the door, running wildly, leaping over boxes as Jefferson ran towards Peters and the gunfire continued.

The sound of the gunshots vibrated in her body, the sound exploding in her middle. Wait... That wasn't sound.

A terrible pain exploded in her side, knocking her to the grimy floor, so cold, so dusty. She felt something wet when she pulled her hand away from her side and saw blood blooming like a red flower on her white blouse.

She closed her eyes for a second, just after seeing their backup team raiding the room, weapons aimed on Peters. She saw a screaming Bella running up to her, falling to the floor beside her. When she opened her eyes again, she saw Bella's hands pressed onto her side. Liv wasn't sure if Bella was trying to comfort her or stop the bleeding. She heard more gunshots, shouts, orders, the snapping of handcuffs. Bella crying, Jefferson screaming her name.

Liv just wanted to fade into unconscious, into a world of oblivion. The pain was so unbearable, she just wanted it to end. So she let herself slide into darkness.

*

Isaac burst through the doors of the cabinet shop just after talking to Maria.

"Have you seen Gideon?" he asked another employee, who pointed him to his boss.

Gideon looked busy, talking with an employee about an order. Maybe he would go call Olivia and then tell Gideon about it after.

"Isaac?" a new employee said as Isaac walked toward the shop phone. "There's a phone call for you."

A phone call? He never got phone calls for him personally. Was something wrong?

Was it Liv?

He rushed to the phone, picking it up.

"Hello? This is Isaac Troyer."

"Isaac, this is Officer Jefferson Martin. I'm afraid I have some bad news for you."

Isaac's knees felt weak as he leaned against the wooden desk, dread filling him like poison.

"Liv has been shot," Jefferson said.

Isaac felt lightheaded. His knees gave out, then he crumpled to the floor, pressing his palm to his forehead. A dozen questions bombarded his brain.

"How bad?" he managed to choke out. "Is she…?"

"No, she's alive. She was shot in the side. She'll recover fully, but I knew you'd want to know. And I didn't know what her family's contact information was or if they have a phone in their house. So I looked up the cabinet company's phone number. Just get them down here and come see her, okay? She'll want to see you."

Isaac squinted his eyes shut, trying to fight off the dizziness, trying to slow his heart rate. She'd be okay. She'd be okay…

"Thanks so much for calling, Officer Martin."

"No problem."

Jefferson gave Isaac Liv's location and hospital room number, then they hung up, and Isaac felt like kicking himself again for not protecting her. He wished he could have been there for her!

He promised himself that would never happen again. He wanted to protect her for the rest of his life. He wanted to always be there for her and love her forever.

He picked himself up off the floor, glad no one else had been in the office. He stumbled out into the shop.

"Gideon?" he called out, looking for Liv's uncle to tell him the news.

*

The Mast family and Isaac piled out of the driver's car when they reached the hospital. Liv was shunned, but because she had solved the crimes in their community and because she had been injured, the bishop and the elders graciously made an exception and allowed the Mast family and Isaac to go see Liv without being shunned themselves.

As they reached Liv's room, they all huddled outside the door.

"You go in first," Isaac told them. "I need a minute, and you're her family."

They agreed and started walking.

"Wait." Isaac grabbed Gideon's arm. "I have something to ask you."

"What is it?" Gideon said, and Mary and Maria gathered around.

He knew this was not the best timing, but he also knew he couldn't go another hour without asking Liv to marry him. "I'd like to ask you for Liv's hand in marriage. I want to ask her to marry me," he blurted, pushing the words out before he got too nervous.

Gideon grabbed Isaac's shoulders and pulled him into a hug. "I'd be so very happy to have you as a son-in-law." Gideon's voice cracked as his eyes filled with joyful tears. "You have our blessing."

Liv was not technically their daughter, but Isaac knew to Mary and Gideon, she was like their own child. And Maria and Liv were like sisters.

"I'm so happy for you!" Maria cried.

"Finally," Aunt Mary said, smiling through her tears.

"But where will you live?" Gideon asked. "Will you be Amish or *Englisher*?"

"Look, that's a whole other conversation. I thank you for your blessing, but now you should go in and see Liv. We will talk about that later."

As they went inside the room, Isaac paced the hall. "Please, God. Give me the right words to say," he prayed quietly. He gripped his worn Bible for comfort, then felt for the small box in his pocket. He had bought the ring that day before coming to the hospital. The Amish did not wear jewelry or even wedding rings, but he wanted Liv to have a ring. Besides, Liv was an *Englisher*.

After what seemed like hours, the Mast family came out into the hallway.

"She's doing well," Mary said, then turned away, her eyes red. "But it is so hard for me to see her like this."

Isaac touched her shoulder, then stepped into the room.

Liv lay on the white hospital bed, looking almost as pale as the sheets. Several monitors and machines hummed and beeped around her. She smiled at him weakly. It broke his heart to see her like this, just like it had hurt Mary.

"Isaac." Her voice was quiet as she reached out for him. He rushed to her side and sat in the chair beside her.

"I'm so sorry I lied to you about not loving you," she murmured as he took her hand gently, careful not to disrupt the IV.

"Shhh. It's all right, Liv. I understand now why you did it. But you shouldn't have felt like you had to make that choice for me." His love for her threatened to burst his chest open.

"I only did it because I love you." He noticed the purple circles under her eyes. "It's stupid, really."

"We'll laugh about it one day." He hoped to laugh with her every day until he died. He picked up his Bible and set it on the bed next to her. "I brought this for you. I know you don't have one with you, and it brought me a lot of comfort when I was in this hospital."

"Thank you so much. You know I wasn't lying about wanting to become closer to God, right?" She patted his hand.

"Good. I'm so glad." He reached out to touch her smooth face. "Liv, I want to help you every step of the way, whenever you need me. In fact, I want to be with you every day for the rest of my life." An overwhelming elation filled him, taking up space in every pore of his body. "I've been thinking a lot about what I would do to be with you, and I realized I would do anything. Even if it meant leaving behind everything I know and love. If marrying you means I have to leave the community, then I will do it."

She looked at him questioningly at first, then a smile covered her face as she remained silent for once. She knew. She knew what was coming.

He stood up, then bent down on one knee, keenly aware of Maria, Mary and Gideon, who were now spying on them conspicuously from the doorway.

"Olivia Mast, you mean more to me than anything else in this life ever could. Will you marry me?" He opened the small box to reveal a sparkling diamond. Liv gasped when she saw it and burst into tears of joy, grinning, unable to say anything. For several moments as he put the ring on her finger, she still said nothing, obviously in complete shock.

"This is the first time I've ever seen you not have some type of smart remark for something." Isaac laughed as he held her hand, waiting for an answer.

She let out a cry of joy. "Yes! I say yes!"

Isaac gently hugged her as the three eavesdroppers ran into the room, laughing and crying all at once, crowding around them.

"It's so beautiful," she told Isaac, pulling him towards her to kiss him.

"Wait, you got her a ring? But we don't wear jewelry," Maria observed.

Isaac looked at Liv. "I decided I am going to live in the *Englisher* world with Liv."

The Mast family gasped. "Even if you are shunned?"

"Yes," Isaac said.

*

After several laughs and tears, the Mast family and Isaac had to go back home.

Liv stared in disbelief at the ring glistening on her finger, a round diamond set on a dainty, antique-looking band. Beyond it she saw the Bible on her lap. She opened it and flipped through its worn, torn, written-on pages. She wondered how many times Isaac had read passages from this Bible, how many hours he had spent in its words. Even though they were apart, Liv felt close to him as she held the book in her hands, then held it to her chest.

Yes, she wanted her relationship with God back. She knew she had to start somewhere, and she knew it was definitely time for her to really talk to Him.

She bent her head, closed her eyes, and prayed aloud quietly.

"God, I know I have ignored You for a long time, but I miss the relationship I used to have with You. I know You never ignored me. It was I who pulled away from You. You say in your Word that You never leave our sides. From now on I want to do Your will and follow You. Thank you for giving me Isaac. I know he will help me grow closer to You and that he will teach me more about You. But help me be diligent in reading Your Word and talking with You. I don't want to ignore You anymore. In Jesus' name, amen."

A sniff came from the doorway and Liv looked up to see the nurse with the short, dark hair crying at the door.

"I'm so sorry," she said, blowing her nose. "I know I'm not supposed to eavesdrop, but that was beautiful."

"Are you a Christian, too?" Liv asked, slightly embarrassed but also touched.

"Well, I used to go to church with my grandmother a long time ago, but I have never heard anyone pray like that. The church I went to was so serious, I never knew you could know God personally like you do." The nurse wiped her teary eyes, stepping closer. "I'd like to know God like that."

"I can tell you how." And she knew she could. "Want me to show you?"

"Oh, yes. I'd love that."

Epilogue

"This is my favorite place to eat," Liv said, unwrapping her sandwich as she sat in her undercover patrol car outside a sandwich shop next to Officer Martin's. "Come on, try it."

Liv glanced at Isaac's badge as he hesitantly unwrapped his lunch. She had to admit, he looked great sporting his new short haircut, which was so different from his usual dark waves.

Isaac took a big bite of his sandwich. "This is good! Much different than the food I grew up eating on the farm."

"I told you you'd like it." She reached out and grabbed his left hand—the one that wore a wedding band. She looked at her own left hand, admiring for the thousandth time the way her rings sparkled in the sunlight.

They had used Liv's vacation time to elope to the Bahamas, where they spent the best fourteen days of their lives snorkeling, swimming, and sitting on a beach. But after a while, Liv got restless, ready to get back to work.

Isaac was training with CPDU Academy to become a police officer. New CPDU officers in Maine completed a 100 hour pre-service course and worked under another officer, so Isaac was working under Officer Martin, because spouses weren't allowed to be partners.

Isaac would attend the Maine Criminal Justice Academy for four months, then he would be certified to work on his own. CPDU also required officers in training to complete a three-month Field Training Officer program in addition to the CPDU Academy after they completed a 40-hour pre-service online program and passed an academy pre-service exam.

Liv had done the same training when she had joined CPDU Academy and had gone through even more training to become a detective.

Isaac was clearly loving his training. While sometimes the other officers, agents, bodyguards, and detectives liked to harmlessly tease him about being a former Amish man, he was already one of the best shots in the entire unit, and everyone knew it. Liv smiled at Isaac proudly.

And even though she missed her relatives, the community was finally safe and peaceful again.

Liv's mind wandered back to when she had visited Diana in prison. She'd been surprised that Diana had agreed to talk with her.

*

"Why did you come here?" Diana asked, getting straight to the point. "I thought I would be the last person you'd want to spend time with."

"Honestly, I am not really sure. I guess I wanted to see how you're doing. How are you?"

"As well as I could be, I suppose." She let out a heavy sigh. "I can't believe you are here after all those things I said to you and about you."

"I forgive you for all that."

"Really? Even for telling you I didn't believe you when you told me Jake was abusing you? Even for trying to make people think you killed him so you could be with Isaac?" Diana's eyes grew wider as she spoke. Her usual sarcastic tone was gone, leaving only sincerity. Maybe the time she had spent in prison had made her rethink everything.

Liv nodded. "But you did believe me, didn't you? You knew what Jake was really like. I could see it in your eyes the day I told you."

Diana looked away, pain shadowing her face as memories furrowed her brows. "Yes. Of course I knew you were telling the truth. He was my son. He was his father's son."

"So why did you lie? Why didn't you help me?" Liv paused and leaned forward, her voice lowering. "Was Bill like Jake?"

Diana looked up slowly. "I never told anyone. I didn't know what to do. But I guess it doesn't matter who knows now. That's why I told you I didn't believe you. I guess I was afraid you would figure out Bill was abusive, too."

"You could have gotten help. We both could have."

"Probably. But I was afraid of what he would do if he found out I told someone." Diana shook her head slowly. "To me, it was easier to continue living that way, enduring that familiar pain rather than venturing into the unknown by doing something about it. He would have killed me if he had found out I told someone." Diana shifted in her chair and continued. "Bill wasn't like any of the other men. You know he wasn't born Amish. He was raised *Englisher,* and his father abused him. His father was an extremely cold and cruel man. Bill continued the cycle with our children. Then he tormented Ian about

Ava's death, all the while knowing none of it was true. He could have just told him that Ava was alive, hidden right in our basement. It must have been so horrible for Ian. But any time I tried to do or say something about it, it only made Bill angrier, which made it worse. I eventually gave up."

Liv's heart ached for the Sullivan family. "I'm so sorry. I can't even imagine how horrible it must have been."

"The worst part was all those years that Ava was locked up in our basement. I keep wishing I had told someone or called the police. But honestly, Bill made me so afraid that I never did. He told me he'd kill the both of us. And I believed him. I thought I was keeping Ava safe. But I was lying to myself. And now I will pay for it the rest of my life." Diana swatted away a tear and bent her head over her folded hands.

"She's brilliant. She told me how you secretly brought her language, theology, psychology, and science textbooks."

"I had to do something for her. I know we aren't allowed to get college educations, but they were only books I found at thrift stores and yard sales. I love her, you know, and I always knew she is smart. It may not seem like it, but I really do love her. I will never forgive myself for letting Bill steal all those years of her life from her. And I will especially never forgive myself for not letting her out after he died, just so I wouldn't go to prison. And look where I am now. I can't believe how cowardly I was."

"You should forgive yourself. And accept God's forgiveness."

She shook her head vigorously. "I can't."

"Maybe you will someday."

"Well, I have plenty of time to contemplate it." Diana let out a flat, lifeless chuckle.

"You probably already know she got a scholarship and is studying to become a counselor."

Diana nodded. "She deserves it. What about Samuel and Ian? Did you visit them too?"

"Well, Samuel refused to see me. As for Ian, I just didn't have the courage to ask to visit him. I'm really working on forgiving him for killing my family. Finding out he did it crushed me all over again. But I know with God's help I will be able to forgive him soon."

"I'm sure you will. You're strong, Liv. I admire you."

Liv felt her face heat with embarrassment. "Thanks."

The security guard came to the door and told her it was time to go.

"Want me to come back sometime?" Liv asked Diana.

She nodded and smiled a weak smile. "I'll have to check my schedule."

"See you soon." Liv got up and walked to the door.

"Liv?"

She turned to see another tear roll down the older woman's cheek. Untold stories of dark memories and her haunted past gathered in Diana's eyes in the form of more unshed tears. "I'm sorry."

One corner of Liv's mouth lifted. "I know, Diana. And I forgive you."

Though Liv was filled with sorrow at the thought of Diana spending the next several years in prison, she was thankful they were now on good terms.

~*~

Liv and Isaac's new life together was indeed off to a wonderful start, but it was not perfect. Unfortunately, Isaac and Liv had been shunned after they had left the community. They knew it would happen, and they had come to accept it. Though she had already been away from her family for the past six years, it still broke her heart that she couldn't speak to them.

Liv smiled at Isaac, who caught her eye and grinned. There was something in his teeth, but she just laughed. He was adorable. They had each other, and that was all that mattered.

Her communication device crackled to life. "Liv," Branson said, "there has been a robbery right down the road from you at Oakdale Drive. We are sending backup. We suspect the intruder is holding a hostage."

Liv crumpled up the wrapper that held her half-eaten sandwich and dropped it into a paper bag. "Copy that." She glanced at Isaac. "You'll have to finish that later. Ready for this?"

"Yes, ma'am!" Isaac got out of her car and returned to Officer Martin's car parked next to them.

Liv threw her car in reverse, backed out, and blazed out of the parking lot, blue lights flashing. Officer Martin and Isaac followed closely behind.

They drove toward the danger, ready to face anything.

*

Note from the author: I hope you enjoyed this story.
The sequel, *Amish Under Fire*, is now available on Amazon!

I would appreciate an honest review for *Undercover Amish* because reviews are actually very important. They help other customers know more about my books. Your opinion matters!

Thank   you!   Please   feel   free   to   email   me   at ashley@ashleyemmaauthor.com. I'd love to talk with you!

Don't forget to visit http://www.AshleyEmmaAuthor.com/to download free Amish books!

About the Author

Ashley Emma knew she wanted to be a novelist for as long as she can remember. She was home schooled and was blessed with the opportunity to spend her time focusing on reading and writing. She began writing books for fun at a young age, completing her first novella at age 12 and writing her first novel at age 14, then publishing it at age 16.

She went on to write eight more manuscripts before age 25 when she also became a multi-bestselling author.

She owns Fearless Publishing House where she helps other aspiring authors achieve their dreams of publishing their own books.

Ashley lives in Maine with her husband and children, and plans on releasing several more books in the near future.

Visit her at ashleyemmaauthor.com or email her at ashley@ashleyemmaauthor.com. She loves to hear from her readers!

Looking for something new to read? Check out Ashley's other books!

Other books by Ashley Emma on Amazon

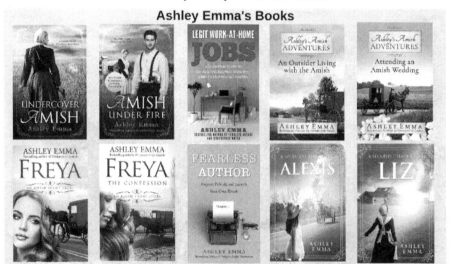

.

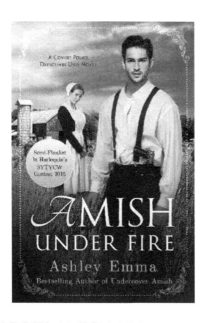

NOW AVAILABLE! AMISH UNDER FIRE

After Maria Mast's abusive ex-boyfriend is arrested for being involved in sex trafficking and modern-day slavery, she thinks that she and her son Carter can safely return to her Amish community.
But the danger has only just begun.
Someone begins stalking her, and they want blood and revenge.
Agent Derek Turner of Covert Police Detectives Unit is assigned as her bodyguard and goes with her to her Amish community in Unity, Maine.
Maria's secretive eyes, painful past, and cautious demeanor intrigue him.
As the human trafficking ring begins to target the Amish community, Derek wonders if the distraction of her will cost him his career…and Maria's life.
Buy here: http://a.co/fT6D7sM

Free eBook!
FREYA: AN AMISH SHORT STORY (Book 1 in the Freya Series)

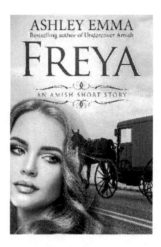

After Freya Wilson accidentally hits an Amish man with her car in a storm, will she have the courage to tell his family the truth—especially after she meets his handsome brother?

Get it free: https://www.amazon.com/Freya-Amish-Short-Ashley-Emma-ebook/dp/B01MSP03UX

New release! FREYA: THE CONFESSION (Book 2 in the Freya
Series)

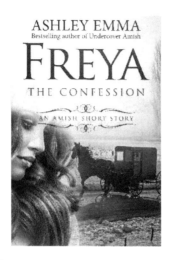

Adam Lapp expected the woman who killed his brother accidentally
with her car to be heartless and cruel. He never expected her to a
timid, kind, and beautiful woman who is running for her life from a
controlling ex who wants her dead.

When Freya Wilson asks him to take her to his family so she can tell
them the truth, he agrees.

Will she find hope in the ashes, or just more darkness and sorrow?

https://www.amazon.com/Freya-Confession-Amish-Short-Forgiveness-
ebook/dp/B076PQF5FS

ASHLEY'S AMISH ADVENTURES: AN OUTSIDER LIVING WITH THE AMISH

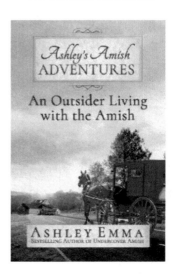

Ever wondered what it would be like to live in an Amish community? Now you can find out in this true story for young adults and middle grade readers.

https://www.amazon.com/Ashleys-Amish-Adventures-Outsider-community-ebook/dp/B01N5714WE

FEARLESS AUTHOR: PREPARE, PUBLISH, AND LAUNCH YOUR OWN
EBOOK
Have you always dreamed of becoming an author?

"…The list of places to promote your book along with the step-by-step publishing and marketing checklist is well worth the cost of this eBook."
---Nicole Cruz, www.nicolecruzproofreader.com
In *Fearless Author*, I will show you how I launched my own bestselling books.
https://www.amazon.com/Fearless-Author-step-step-self-publishing-ebook/dp/B06XJGRRT1

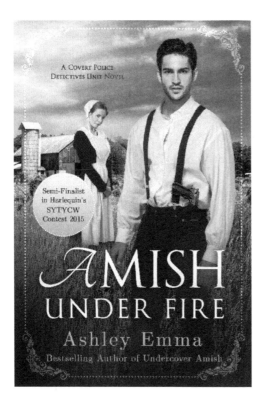

Amish Under Fire excerpt

Maria Mast waited in line at her bank in Portland, Maine, wearing a nametag printed with the word *Kate* and a retro waitress uniform she couldn't wait to change out of. She removed the nametag and tucked it away before anyone else could see it. The back of the dress advertised Miss Portland's Diner, and now she cringed at the thought of people knowing where she worked. The dining car restaurant looked as though it was straight out of the '40s with its marble countertops, hardwood booths and lively patterns. She should have thrown on a jacket to hide the words on the back of her dress before entering the bank.

Kate was not her real name. Maria had to lie to her boss about a lot of things, but she was grateful for Maureen, the benevolent woman who had given her a job and hadn't asked too many questions. Her boss hadn't asked why Maria had shown up for her interview with bruises on her arms or why she didn't even talk to anyone about her personal life. She didn't ask why Maria didn't make friends or trust anyone. Maureen even pretended not to notice when Maria would glance up nervously every time she heard the loud rumbling of a diesel truck pulling into the parking lot.

Even if Maureen could have seen the gun concealed under Maria's uniform skirt, Maria wondered if her boss would have even pressed for information about that.

The bank teller beckoned to her, and Maria slid her cash toward the woman wearing round spectacles. Just after depositing the money, she heard the doors open and screams erupt throughout the busy bank.

She whirled around. Two armed masked men in all black entered the building.

"Everybody on the ground!" the first criminal shouted while the other stomped over to the tellers, demanding cash.

Maria lowered herself to the ground along with everyone else. Maria's heart fell into her stomach, and anxiety constricted her throat and chest. Maybe if everyone did what the men said, no one would get hurt.

Or maybe she would die here, today, after surviving everything she had already been through. Though she was only twenty-five, she had already endured more hardship than some people did over an entire lifetime.

She considered the gun strapped to her leg and wondered what to do. What if she accidentally hit an innocent bystander?

A man who had been waiting in line a few people behind her was wearing some type of security guard uniform with a gun strapped to his hip. The man's hand automatically went to his gun.

"Hey! What are you, a cop?" one of the robbers asked before the man could even get the gun out of his holster. "You shoot and

I'll kill somebody." The bank robber aimed his massive gun at a sobbing bank teller. "Give me the gun, or she dies." The robber's eyes burned with a compassionless fire.

The man in the uniform reluctantly removed the pistol from its holster and handed it slowly to the bank robber. Defeat and indignation darkened his face as he sank to the ground beside the others.

The gunman forced the weeping bank teller to hand over all of the cash available.

"That's all the cash we have!" the harried teller with the spectacles cried when the bank robber demanded more cash.

"There's got to be more!" he shouted.

"No, I swear, that's all of it!"

The gunmen grabbed a little girl by the wrist, wrenching her away from her mother as she screamed in terror. He locked her under his arm and held the gun to her head.

"If you don't get me the rest of the cash, I'll blow a hole through her head!" he screamed at the teller.

Maria's muscles tensed with every word he shouted. She had to do something.

Her heart pounding harder with each passing second, her fingers reached up to her knee where her M&P Shield was secured in its holster. She slid it out and rested her forefinger along the side of the gun and clicked off the safety.

The man in the law enforcement uniform caught her eye, looked at the gun, and gave her a nod. His eyes communicated to hers behind black-rimmed rectangle glasses. When she hesitated, he nodded again and jerked his head ever so slightly to the robbers.

Somehow she knew he had a plan. He would help her. All they had to do was create enough chaos for it to work.

"Look, the police!" the man shouted, his outburst making the two gunmen turn to the window in a panic.

In the two seconds of time he gave her, she aimed and fired, hitting the first gunman by the door in the leg.

The man with the glasses lunged toward the other gunman who held the girl, knocking her out of the way, and after they moved, Maria hit that gunman in the leg also.

Two other men who had been in line leapt into action, swiping the weapons from the two robbers and restraining them as their screams of pain filled the air.

The hours spent at the shooting range had paid off. She had traded some of her paintings for shooting lessons, and her instructor had told her she was a natural.

The man with the glasses looked over at her, admiration radiating from him to her.

The rest of the people in the bank turned to her, thanking her. Especially the girl's mother, who ran to her crying, throwing her arms around her in a hug.

What if this was reported on the news? What if her face got on TV?

After all her hard work, *he* would find her. This time, Maria didn't know if he would let her live.

She had to get out of there. She pried the girl's mother's hands off her and made a beeline for the door, then slammed into someone.

Two strong hands steadied her as she looked up into the face of the handsome Glasses Man.

"I'm Derek Turner, an agent of CPDU. I don't usually wear a uniform, but I was on security duty today for an event. I usually have my gun concealed. So it's a good thing you were here. Though you don't look like the type of person who would carry a concealed weapon. That's none of my business, I guess. Where did you learn to shoot like that?"

"I took lessons at a range. Look, I have a concealed weapons permit." Maria pulled the permit out of her wallet and handed it to him. "I just want to be able to defend myself." She wriggled out of his grasp.

"You just saved that girl's life, and we now have the criminals under control. So what's wrong?" he asked, peering into her eyes, too close for comfort. His dark hair was gelled stylishly above a short, stubbly beard, and as he looked into her eyes, she felt as though he could see all of her secrets.

Everything, she wanted to say.

***

"I need everyone in the situation room, please," Captain Branson of the Covert Police Detectives Unit in Augusta, Maine, bellowed. Several special agents, bodyguards, detectives, and police officers looked up from what they had been doing.

"Now!"

Everyone started moving more quickly at Branson's sharp tone. Agent Derek Turner had just sat down at his desk to make a few reports from an arrest he had made earlier that day. Now it would have to wait. When Branson said 'now,' he meant *now*. All the officers, analysts and agents milled into the situation room.

Branson cleared his throat as everyone quieted down. "We have received some information on a sex trafficking ring in Portland. We think it might be the same ring that moves from Boston to Portland we tried to shut down four years ago."

Derek remembered the case well. CPDU had managed to arrest several of the traffickers, but most of them, along with the boss of the trafficking ring, had relocated themselves as well as all the girls they had kidnapped, and then the trail had gone cold.

It was the same sex ring that was the cause of his wife's death. Anger and grief roiled in Derek's stomach, but he clenched his fists and tried to focus on what Branson was saying.

"We think the ring has returned to Portland, possibly after relocating to Boston. We received a tip from someone at the Maine Mall. They suspect that there are young men who are luring in teenage girls by flattering them, spending time with them at the mall, and then offering to drive them home or to a movie. Instead, the men just bring them to the trafficking headquarters. Four girls have gone missing this month at the mall alone." Branson pointed to four photos that had been hung up, all of men in their twenties. "We have identified these three men from mall security footage talking to teenage girls multiple times, but we have not located them yet. Garret Fletcher, Ryan Thompson, and Trevor Monroe. We need to be on the lookout for them. If you see any of them, do not arrest them. We need to follow them so that they can hopefully lead us to their temporary headquarters if they are indeed working for the ring."

Derek studied the photos, and one of the agents passed copies around the room to everyone.

Branson tugged on the belt that was snug under his round belly. "I will assign four agents to go undercover on a mission. We think the traffickers might be keeping the girls temporarily somewhere in Portland. We are trying to pinpoint the location. I am assigning four men to pose as potential 'buyers' while gathering information undercover." Branson made quotation marks with his fingers, making no effort to hide his disgust.

Rage against the traffickers boiled Derek's own blood, but he listened intently as Branson continued.

"Cristman, Banks, Rogers, and Smith, I will tell you the details of the mission after this meeting."

As Branson continued speaking, Derek tried to listen, but he slowly tuned Branson out, memories taking over his mind. The blood on the white carpet of his apartment, the blood on the walls, Natalia's bruised body lying skewed and broken on the floor...

He had been too late to save her. He'd been working when the murder occurred, trying to locate the very traffickers who had been in his own home that night, targeting the love of his life.

The obscene message written on the wall in her blood had been enough evidence to tell them this specific ring had committed the murder out of revenge after Derek had arrested several of their traffickers. Witnesses had also seen the traffickers in the apartment building on the night of the murder.

But they had disappeared, and CPDU hadn't had any significant clues to their whereabouts.

Until now.

Everyone stood up, and Derek silently chided himself. The meeting was over, and he had zoned out. He hoped he didn't miss any important information. He'd ask one of the others about it later.

Wait. He hadn't been chosen to go on the mission. He was one of the best field agents in the unit. Why hadn't Branson chosen him? Annoyed, he maneuvered his six-foot frame through the people trying to leave the room and walked up to the captain.

"You're wondering why I didn't pick you for this assignment," Captain Branson said gruffly, turning to Derek and looking up at him.

"Yes, sir. Is it something I did? I'm just wondering why."

"No, Turner. It's not anything you did wrong. It's just... The mission will take place on the fourth anniversary of your wife's death. I didn't want you to be distracted, that's all. You are human, just like the rest of us, and distractions can lead to fatal mistakes," Branson said, sidling past him. "Remember two years ago?"

Derek nodded solemnly. He had been so distracted by grief that he had almost let a suspect escape custody. "That was then. I won't make the same mistake again."

"I know you want the same thing as everyone else, which is to catch these guys. So I need you to do something else."

"Yes, sir," Derek felt defeated, but he accepted his captain's decision. If Branson thought this was best, then Derek would comply.

"A woman just walked in here, Maria Mast, the woman who shot those two bank robbers. She claims her ex-boyfriend is abusing her, and he is one of the traffickers we saw on the mall security footage who is kidnapping teenage girls, Trevor Monroe. Maria is Detective Olivia Troyer's cousin, who has been temporarily transferred to work on a case. Go talk to her and get as much information from her as you can. Let's arrest this trafficker," Branson said, tugging on his belt once more, his bald head gleaming in the light from the ceiling. "See if she can help us find out where the headquarters is. She might know where Monroe is. Report to me afterward. Go."

Branson turned to the four agents he had picked and began discussing the details of the mission.

When he saw that his friend Agent Ben Banks was one of the chosen, Derek could not deny that he felt a twinge of jealousy. They had worked together for a few years now. Banks was good in the field, but Derek knew he was even better. Even though he was only twenty-nine, Derek already had more experience than many of the other agents, thanks to his service in the military.

This didn't seem fair. Now Derek was stuck gathering information and pushing papers while his coworkers got to do the really important work.

He told himself to get over it as he walked to the front of the building to take the woman into his office. He stepped into the waiting room and said, "Maria Mast?"

A young boy was holding a coloring book and the woman's hand, his brown eyes glancing around behind his round glasses, taking in CPDU with fascination. Derek smiled, then he looked at the boy's mother.

The slender young woman walked toward him. Her long hair was highlighted a lovely shade of honey blonde, falling in loose curls that framed her beautiful face. She wore a simple gray sweater dress that might as well have been a ball gown, it looked so wonderful on her. As she walked, her black heels clacking on the marble floor. She appeared to be a few years younger than him, maybe in her mid-twenties. However, her brown eyes held fear, hurt and secrets beyond her years, and that intrigued Derek.

She was a sight to behold.

Speak, you fool, he told himself when she looked at him expectantly.

But his mind drew a blank.

To be continued…

Amish Under Fire is now available on Amazon!

45805741R00177

Made in the USA
Lexington, KY
19 July 2019